"LANGUAGE" P(

"LANGUAGE" POETRIES

AN ANTHOLOGY

Edited with an introduction by Douglas Messerli

A New Directions Book

Grateful thanks are given to the authors and their publishers for permission to reprint the following works:

Bruce Andrews. "While," "And the Love of Laughter," and "Matter of Fact," from *Wobbling* (Copyright © 1981 by Bruce Andrews), Roof Books; "Confidence Trick," from *Give Em Enough Rope* (Copyright © 1986 by Bruce Andrews), Sun & Moon Press.

Rae Armantrout. "Extremities," from *Extremities* (Copyright © 1978 by Rae Armantrout), The Figures; "Double," "Latter Day," and "Through Walls," from *Precedence* (Copyright © 1985 by Rae Armantrout), Burning Deck; "Necromance" and "Range" (Copyright © 1987 by Rae Armantrout).

Charles Bernstein. "Senses of Responsibility," from *Senses of Responsibility* (Copyright © 1979 by Charles Bernstein), Tuumba Press; "Sentences My Father Used," from *Controlling Interests* (Copyright © 1980, 1986 by Charles Bernstein), Roof Books; "Stove's Out," from *Stigma* (Copyright © 1981 by Charles Bernstein), Station Hill Press; "You," from *Resistance* (Copyright © 1983 by Charles Bernstein), Awede Press.

Clark Coolidge. "The Death of Floyd Collins," from *Flag Flutter and U.S. Electric* (Copyright © 1966 by Clark Coolidge), Lines: "Fed Drapes," from *Space* (Copyright © 1970 by Clark Coolidge), Harper & Row Publishers, Inc.; excerpts from *The Maintains* (Copyright © 1974 by Clark Coolidge), This Press; "Manlius to Coeymans" and "Album—A Runthru," from *Own Face* (Copyright © 1978 by Clark Coolidge), Angel Hair; excerpts from *Mine: The One That Enters the Stories* (Copyright © 1982 by Clark Coolidge), The Figures; "Thin Places" and "I drove through this old world this afternoon," from *Solution Passage: Poems 1978-1981* (Copyright © 1986 by Clark Coolidge), Sun & Moon Press.

Tina Darragh. Selections from *On the Corner to Off the Corner* (Copyright © 1981 by Tina Darragh), Sun & Moon Press; "ludicrous stick," in *The Paris Review* #86 (Copyright © 1982 by The Paris Review).

Alan Davies. "Shared Sentences," from *Active Hours* (Copyright © 1982 by Alan Davies), Roof Books; excerpts from *Name* (Copyright © 1986 by Alan Davies), This Press.

Ray DiPalma. "The Bed," from *Two Poems* (Copyright © 1982 by Ray DiPalma); "Hadrian's Lane" in *The Paris Review* #86 (Copyright © 1982 by The Paris Review); "Ripe Tack," "Poem," "The Table," and "The Anecdote That Went with It (Copyright © 1987 by Ray DiPalma).

Ted Greenwald. Selections from *Common Sense* (Copyright © 1978 by Ted Greenwald), L Publications.

Diane Ward. Selections from *Never Without One* (Copyright © 1984 by Diane Ward), Roof Books.

Hannah Weiner. Excerpts from *Spoke* (Copyright © 1984 by Hannah Wiener), Sun & Moon Press.

Manufactured in the United States of America
First published clothbound and as New Directions Paperbook 630 in 1987
Published simultaneously in Canada by Penguin Books Canada Ltd.

Library of Congress Cataloging-in-Publication Data

"Language" poetries.
    Bibliography: p. 179.
    1.   American poetry—20th century.   I.   Messerli, Douglas, 1947–
PS615.L29   1987   811'.5408   86-18173
ISBN 0-8112-1006-5
ISBN 0-8112-1007-3 (pbk.)

New Directions Books are published for James Laughlin
by New Directions Publishing Corporation,
80 Eighth Avenue, New York 10011

CONTENTS

Introduction by Douglas Messerli   1

Jackson Mac Low   13
Hannah Weiner   23
Susan Howe   29
Clark Coolidge   41
Lyn Hejinian   52
Ted Greenwald   62
Peter Seaton   69
Michael Palmer   74
Ray DiPalma   83
James Sherry   94
Rae Armantrout   101
P. Inman   108
Bob Perelman   114
Bruce Andrews   121
Barrett Watten   131
Charles Bernstein   143
Tina Darragh   156
Alan Davies   159
Carla Harryman   166
Diane Ward   172

Bibliographical Information   179

Introduction

In a decade in which so many poets and critics have expressed dismay over an ever-shrinking audience for contemporary poetry and have decried what they see as a decline in the cultural and political vitality of poetry and poetics, we have also witnessed something else: an almost meteoric rise in the publications and readership of the poets associated with what has come to be called "Language" writing, and an equal rise in the critical attention paid to them. Since 1976, poets associated in one way or another with this group have published over 150 books of poetry and criticism—demonstrating a resourcefulness and energetic re-thinking of the nature of poetry both in social and aesthetic terms. Such an output would be astonishing in any literary period, but is nearly miraculous in light of the doomsayers' predictions of the death of poetry as we know it.

Admittedly, the readership for many of these publications is small, sometimes verging on the coterie. But dozens of these books have reached a larger audience, and several of these poets can find their works in bookshops from Boise, Idaho, to Coral Gables, Florida, and in classrooms from the University of Maine to the California Institute of Technology. And as a publisher of and poet associated with this group, I have increasingly encoun-tered general readers, students, and professors who, cornering me, ask: "But tell us, what *is* 'Language' poetry?"

That question, whether friendly or hostile, delivers to the muscles of my back and shoulders a slight flinch. How much it presumes!—that there is a single definition or a unified complex of ideas which applies to "Language" poetry, and underlying that assumption, that there is an identifiable group of poets which can be described as writing whatever one defines "Lan-guage" writing as being.

It may be tempting to begin an answer to such a question by taking the familiar historical approach and describing certain general influences and sources of several "Language" poets. Certainly the work of Gertude Stein and the writings of the Russian Futurists and *zaum* poets like Velimir Khlebnikov and Alexi Khruchonykh immediately come to mind as touchstones for the work of "Language" writers as diverse as Charles Bernstein, P. Inman, Bruce Andrews, Barrett Watten, Hannah Weiner, and Lyn Hejinian. But other than recognizing that Stein and the Futurists grounded their work in the notion of language as the engenderer of experience and often structured their poetry in terms of a linguistic play of words and ideas, this history really doesn't tell us much. If we probe any further, we find that, while for some "Language" poets (Susan Howe, for example) a major figure may be Emily Dickinson, others (such as Bernstein) may claim models in the poetry of Robert Creeley, Louis Zukofsky, and Thomas Campion! Add to this the fact that for the "Language" poets in general major sources of inspiration have been found in politics and social theory, philosophy, psychology, painting and sculpture, film, and dance, and one perceives that any definition by association becomes ridiculous. Encyclopedic in their interests, these poets are as likely to be "influenced" by the work of their peers and cultural events as by any one "literary" tradition.

Still, quite naturally, one seeks a shared aesthetic, a body of ideas about poetry and poetics that has shaped these far-embracing poets into a group of sorts in the 1970s and 1980s. And certainly there are values and attitudes toward poetry that these poets share. The poets in this anthology have all foregrounded language itself as the project of their writing. For these poets, language is not something that *explains* or *translates* experience, but is the source of experience. Language is perception, thought itself; and in that context the poems of these writers do not function as "frames" of experience or brief narrative summaries of ideas and emotions as they do for many current poets. Communication, as Bernstein writes, is seen not as a "two-way wire with the message shuttling back and forth in blissful ignorance of the (its) transom (read: ideology)," but as "a sounding of language from the inside, in which the dwelling is already / always given."[1] What I call "portmanteau poetry"—poetry that, revealing its message to the reader, is used up and closed until the reader again seeks such feelings or knowledge—such poetry is rejected in favor of the production of a living document of the author's engagement with the reader and the world through language as the agent of their shared thinking. The poem, accordingly, exists, as Bernstein has observed, "in a matrix of social and historical relations that are more significant to the formation of an individual text than any personal qualities of the life or voice of an author."[2]

While these writers thus participate in the climate of the poetics of Charles Olson's process-oriented writing ("one perception must must must MOVE, INSTANTER, ON ANOTHER!")[3] and the disjunctive procedures of the poets associated with the New York School, they have eschewed the myth-making and personalization of poetry practiced by these and other modern poets. Writing, rather, becomes for most of them a political action in which the reader is not required merely to read or listen *to* the poem but is asked to participate *with* the poet/poem in bringing meaning to the community at large. As Craig Watson has concluded, such writing serves as "a performance in which the reader is both audience and performer."[4]

The demand that the reader function less as a sounding board than sound with the poet upon and inside the poem requires, in turn, a new kind of reading. The poets in this collection ask for a reading in which meaning, whether understood as a curative or entertainment, is not self-contained like a cold capsule or jellybean, but is inseparable from the language in process—the transformation of phoneme into word, the association of one word to the next, the slip of phrase against phrase, the forward movement and reversal of the sentence—the way one experiences life itself.

Beyond these generalizations, however, these poets and their works resist categorization as to how and what specifically the language means. Surely one might expect to find that Charles Bernstein and Bruce Andrews, the co-editors of *L=A=N=G=U=A=G=E*—the magazine that helped to name this "movement"—share basic notions about how language functions in their work. And in fact there are a great many ideas shared by the two poets. Bernstein argues, for example, that such writing, "rather than making the language as transparent as possible" moves toward denseness and opacity in order to "actually map the fullness of thought and its movement."[5] One recognizes a similar position in Bruce Andrews' call for a poetry in which signifiers "provide echoes, harmonies, overtones, but not the principles of organization"; for a ". . . confusion of realms, profusion of events and interplay on the surface"; for a poetry in which the "subject" disappears "behind the words only to emerge in front, or inside them."[6]

Both Andrews and Bernstein work for a poetry that, while mapping consciousness, does not appear as a "trace" (Bernstein) of the self upon the text or an individual "ownership" (Andrews) of the text. Instead, the poem is understood as a social "work for the reader's . . . projection/construction"[7]: "Language work," writes Andrews, "resembles a creation of a community and of a world-view by a once divided-but-now-fused Reader and Writer."[8]

Yet even here, in discussing some of the basic premises of "Language" writing, Bernstein and Andrews can point in different directions. Andrews argues consistently for sense emerging from an "interplay on the surface" of the poem rather than along a "vertical axis" in which meaning takes place largely "below the plane, out of sight, or earshot." Bernstein—while agreeing with Andrews' disdain for imposed symbols and "hidden layers"—speaks just as consistently for a sounding in poetry approaching music, which, in turn, allows the poem a depth of meanings. If Andrews positions himself as a writer who would make his poetry a public production, creating in "plain sight (and plainsong)" a writing that moves "along a surface with all the complications of a charter or a townmeeting,"[9] Bernstein advocates a concept of privacy for writing that

allows the formal requirements of clarity and exposition to drop away. To speak intimately is to be free to speak as one will, not as one should. Confusion, contradiction, obsessiveness, associative reasoning, etc., are given free(er) play. A semblance of coherence—or

strength or control—drops away. In contrast to this, or taking the
idea further, the private can also seem to be the incommunicable.
As if I had these private sensations (or thoughts or feelings) that no
one can truly know as I know them.[10]

Indeed, Bernstein argues that this concept of the incommuni-
cable is illusory because "language itself is a communality, a
public domain." What this foregrounding of the private actually
does, he posits, is to reveal the public. Andrews, on the other
hand, believes that "a hollowing out of lower depths" and "laby-
rinthine caves of signification" can occur "within the gaps."
Nonetheless, Andrews' search to discover "How communal can
you get?" leads his poetry and theory in a very different direction
from Bernstein's call for a dramatization of a "far-inness."[11]
There is behind most of Andrews' writing a brilliantly aphoristic
voice, a showing of the way—as labyrinthine or "far-out" as that
path may be—as opposed to a more ruminative and sophistical
one (in the sense of arguing publicly for a kind of private logic)
manifested in much of Bernstein's writing.

Thus while they share the social project of foregrounding
language as the medium of consciousness, Andrews and Bern-
stein create very different kinds of poetries, which may begin
with similar premises but produce quite different results.

Similar distinctions might be made between the poetry and
poetics of the co-editors of the San Francisco-based *Poetics Jour-
nal*, Barrett Watten and Lyn Hejinian. In his major book of
criticism, *Total Syntax*, Watten argues less for a particular aes-
thetic point of view as for a "discussion of writing that leads to
what can be done." Accordingly, Watten's essays do not focus on
the poet's ideas or psychology but on presenting a variety of ways
in which twentieth-century authors and artists—with whom Wat-
ten and, by extension, his audience feel some sympathy—have
dealt with such problems as method, style, technique, and social
scale. The self of Watten's criticism (much as he describes in his
essay on "The Politics of Poetry" the two extremes of techniques
used by the contributors to $L=A=N=G=U=A=G=E$ magazine) is
mediated by "the commonsense functionalism of a professional

role" (in Watten's case, this is expressed in his summaries of literary history) and by an "exploded self," a self that is subsumed in the language and theory he treats. And in this sense, there is a presumptive quality—in the best sense of the meaning—in most of Watten's critical writing; as a "kind of thinking . . . done in front of a community of writers,"[12] Watten's critical pieces presume and solicit a certain range of shared values. Thus, a side-by-side presentation of two different approaches can itself function as a pointing; there is no need for an "explanation" that evaluates. Much like Andrews' horizontal presentation of information "with all the complications of a charter or a town-meeting," Watten's criticism—often first presented as "talks"—finds its meaning not in a plumbing of the private self and its values but "within the gaps" filled in by the actively thinking community.

This opening up of the signifying process directly affects his poetry, in that the structure of many of his works, as he notes in his essay "On Explanation," is based upon this process of laying out different techniques and ideas side by side. In "Artifacts," for example, Watten presents different languages "in terms of the essential conflicts within and between them."[13] Thus, he contends, "various explanations on widely different scales interact, forcing language to a new scale of discourse that includes all the possible conflicts. . . ." The "self" of this poem—as in many of Watten's poems—as the engenderer of the structure is given over to and "exploded" by the collision of forms through which language and meaning is reconstituted.

> To produce myself,
> > a dialogue. . . .
> Fixing a voice as it coheres
> > On the page,
> > > to be adjusted
> > I go away and return later
> A distance that equals results. . . .

> > > > (from *Progress*, p. 118)

In "If Written Is Writing" (1978), Lyn Hejinian, Watten's co-editor, appears to share his notion of the "exploded" self: "In such are we obsessed with our own lives, which lives being now language, the emphasis has moved." And in a short piece, published one year later in $L=A=N=G=U=A=G=E$, Hejinian, paralleling Watten's thinking, writes of her interest in a structure of "putting things together in such a way as to enable them to coincide. . . . Like the natural order elsewhere, things can't be seen in ones alone, make twos. Twos and more, too. I am interested in that."[14]

For Hejinian, this coincidence produces a new relationship, which is at once the heart of communal sharing and a movement toward the centric; by giving up the self *to* language, one discovers in the language of the community a new self, a notion quite similar to Watten's "going away" to "return later."

Yet for Hejinian, there are different sources of centricities. One, in which bibliography becomes text, in which "the writing emerges from within a pre-existent text of one's own devising or another's," is that in which the process is "composition rather than writing." We can trace this distinction to Gertrude Stein's "Composition as Explanation," in which Stein develops the idea that what is interesting to people in writing is not what is "inside" them but lies in what is seen, which, in turn, is dependent upon the community that determines the context.[15]

These ideas are very close to Watten's as expressed in the structure of his essays, in which evaluation does not emanate from the "inside," from the author, but from the listeners/viewers, who contextualize and (re)constitute the value of the experience.

But Hejinian also projects another source of centricity in writing that is, in fact, closer to Stein's and Hejinian's own work. In this other source, "one locates in the interior texture of such language as is of the person composing from it, personal and inclusive. This is not necessarily 'self-revelatory,'" she argues, but is built up through patterns of language, "relevant quirks," "concentration, condensation, deconstruction, and such as association by, for example, pun and etymology provide: an allusive pyscholinguism."[16]

Here, in fact, one perceives an aesthetic closer to Bernstein's "privacy" and "far-inness" than to Andrews' outward social horizon or Watten's compositional presentation of different languages.

Again, a similar focus yields quite different results. While she uses programmatic procedures in several of her poems, Hejinian's poetry often presents a linguistic self so private that it forces the reader to enter the poem and (re)construct meaning.

Even within a shared focus, one recognizes a bewildering variety of aesthetic possibilities, of methods to bring reader and writer through language to experience and reconstruct meaning together. When one further puts this in the context of several dozen writers actively involved over a span of more than a decade, the identity of "Language" writing itself is less of a fixed point than an "exploded self." In short, as Charles Bernstein explains in an interview with Tom Beckett, "Language" writing "is not a movement in the traditional art sense, since the value of giving an aesthetic line such profile seems counterproductive to the inherent value of the work."[17]

It is to the social context, then, that one must turn to find any real coherence in this "group." Particularly in San Francisco, and to a somewhat lesser degree in New York and Washington, D.C., the "Language" poets—despite obvious differences in aesthetics—came together out of what Lyn Hejinian has called "motivated coincidence" to provide each other the dialogue and stimulus necessary to create vital and intelligent poetry. Through readings, discussions, seminars, personal friendships, and magazines (such as *Tottel's, Hills, L=A=N=G=U=A=G=E, A Hundred Posters, This, Roof, The Difficulties,* and *Poetics Journal*), they have built up a true community of thought that must be the desire of any poet not writing a hermetic verse for his or her eyes alone.

Obviously, there are problems here as well. As Charles Bernstein has suggested in his essay "The Conspiracy of 'US,'" every "we" creates the danger that the "task" will be avoided by setting up "boundaries" that shield or insulate rather than challenge.[18] In every such group, moreover, there are those who would speak for the others, those who would define restrictions where previously there were none. A great danger for any such group—and one now increasingly facing the "Language" poets—is that once identified with the group, individual poets can be classified—praised or dismissed—simply on the basis of their affiliation. Within the context of the aesthetic differences, this is a particularly disturbing phenomenon with which any "Language" poet must struggle.

But despite these dilemmas, such social gathering has helped not only to gain an initial readership for the individual poets but also to create an atmosphere in which thoughtful and serious writing, an emotional and powerful poetry could be created. In truth, poetry "as we knew it"—the poem that functions as a sort of narrative snapshot of experience, by the poet who sees himself or herself—as Louis Simpson recently described his position —as a worker who, separated from ideas (the abstract), creates a primary product (like a coalminer digging coal) which when brought to surface represents "real" experience[19]—perhaps these notions of poet and poem will not survive. Perhaps it does take a community of concerned thinkers to keep poetry/language alive as the substance of experience, of meaning.

The poems in this anthology are representative of that larger community. The emphasis here is not on aesthetic concerns as much as upon poems that challenge and energize our reading. It is an extreme understatement to say that this short anthology can even begin to represent the diversity and quality of the many voices of this poetic community. When I think of all the other excellent poets I might have included and how much larger is the range of voices than is here represented, I am reminded of David Antin's quip: "Anthologies are to poets what zoos are to animals." What one hopes, what I have worked for, is a selection provocative enough that it sends its readers out to bookstores, libraries, and public readings in search of other "Language" work.[20]

Any such undertaking always is the work of many. The poets included in these pages have all helped directly to create this anthology. And Bruce Andrews, Charles Bernstein, Lyn Hejinian, Susan Howe, James Sherry, and Barrett Watten have spent a great many hours with me sharing ideas, information, and advice. Ron Silliman challenged me in his critiques to question some of my assumptions and to expand the context of the anthology I had first envisioned. Anyone undertaking such a task, finally, should have a supporter as fervent, well-spoken, and intelligent as I had in Marjorie Perloff.

Douglas Messerli

N O T E S

1 Charles Bernstein, introduction to "Language Sampler," *Paris Review*, No. 86 (Winter 1982), 75.

2 Bernstein, "An Interview with Tom Beckett," *Content's Dream: Essays 1975–1984* (Los Angeles: Sun & Moon Press, 1986), p. 408.

3 Charles Olson, "Projective Verse," in Donald M. Allen and Warren Tallman, eds., *The Poetics of the New American Poetry* (New York: Grove Press, 1973), p. 149.

4 Craig Watson, "The Project of Language," *Credences*, III (Fall 1985), 160.

5 Bernstein, "Thought's Measure," *Content's Dream*, p. 70.

6 Bruce Andrews, "Text and Context," Bruce Andrews and Charles Bernstein, eds., *The L=A=N=G=U=A=G=E Book* (Carbondale: Southern Illinois University Press, 1984), pp. 31-38.

7 Bernstein, "Writing and Method," *Content's Dream*, p. 233.

8 Andrews, "Text and Context," p. 35.

9 *Ibid.*, p. 33.

10 Bernstein, "Thought's Measure," p. 80.

11 Bernstein, "Three or Four Things I Know About Him," *Content's Dream*, p. 29.

12 Barrett Watten, *Total Syntax* (Carbondale: Southern Illinois University Press, 1985), p. ix.

13 *Ibid.*, p. 222.

14 Lyn Hejinian, "Smatter," *L=A=N=G=U=A=G=E*, No. 8 (June 1979), [17].

15 See Gertrude Stein, "Composition as Explanation," Patricia Meyerowitz, ed., *Writings and Lectures 1909–1945* (Baltimore: Penguin, 1967) pp. 21–22.

16 Hejinian, "If Written Is Writing," *L=A=N=G=U=A=G=E Book*, p. 30.

17 Bernstein, "An Interview with Tom Beckett," p. 386.

18 Bernstein, "The Conspiracy of 'US,'" *Content's Dream*, p. 344.

19 Based on comments of Louis Simpson, presented at the 11th Alabama Symposium on English and American Literature, "What Is a Poet?" University of Alabama, Tuscaloosa, on October 19, 1984. Collected as *What Is a Poet?*, Hank Lazar, ed. (Tuscaloosa: University of Alabama, 1986).

20 One book, in particular, should be the first on any such reader's list: Ron Silliman's anthology, *In the American Tree*, which encompasses some of the same poets and others in a context larger than these pages could afford. Because of his editing of his own anthology, Silliman opted not to participate in *"Language" Poetries*.

JACKSON MAC LOW

25th Dance—Saying Things About
Making Gardens—22 March 1964

Everyone begins making thunder though taking pigs some-
 where,
& then everyone says something after a minute.

After that everyone's a fly,
having an example.

Pretty soon everyone's giving gold cushions or seeming to do so,
& everyone's crying
& letting something be made the same as something simple
& seeming to send things or putting wires on things,
& everyone's saying things tiredly,
& everyone's taking opinions
& being a band or acting like a bee
& letting things be equal or doing things like an ant
& having curves or having to put weight on a bird,
& everyone's saying things about making gardens.

When all that's over, everyone goes about & comes across art.

A little later everyone reasons regularly.

Still later everyone plants.

Then everyone meets someone over water
& says things tiredly
& takes some more opinions
while making the stomach let itself down,
& again being a band or acting like a bee,
having curves or having to put weight on a bird,
everyone then gets feeble.

That's when everyone makes drinks
though everyone's being earth
& willing themselves to be dead or coming to see something
    narrow.

Can everyone then do something in the manner of a sister whose
    mind is happy & willing
& have uses among harmonies
& finally get insects?

Wall Rev

    A line is a crack
    is an entrance furrow
    distracting between thighs

    Attracting between sighs
    a parallel cataclysm
    cannot tell its name

    Active well of flame
    tense entrance clues
    obligate avoidance

8 December 1981
New York

Giant Otters

They were a close family of giant otters
in Surinam giving a low growling sound when
they were insecure so they were called the Hummers.

Trace elements had landed near them and they effloresced
in even amounts throughout an even eon and an evening more
fortunate as they were in knowing nothing

or peering curiously into unknowable presence
alert to no future living the past as presence
whose elements were traces in their efflorescing being

going as far as they could within the world they were
as fortune particularized occasions within unfolding
breathed upon by memory's wraith and anticipation's all but
    absence.

Where were they going but farther along and through
whatever their being eventuated in clearness no
    demand for clarity
as the eyes are unsealed and the world flows in as light?

13-14 February 1982
New York

Recommend

Annex no next time or anxiety or brood or bid
a last time by silent calculation or a trusted elite
left floundering by unbearable limitations sunk in sequences

a mute filiality opposes and approves as a first mover moves
though autumn's over and the sly defeat the cunning
running farther when leaves greet in octave show.

11 February 1982
New York

Trope Market

In the network, in the ruin,
flashing classics gravitate,
snared, encumbered voicelessly.

Teak enticements seek, leaping
fan-shaped arras corners
snore among in backward dispatch.

Panels glow, groan, territorialize
fetishistically in nacreous
instantaneity spookily shod.

4 July 1983
New York

Various Meanings

The bottom of a green arras extends a vocabulary
whose rest is deep and boundless moving through space
and the stars. From time to time we lost the noise of an edge
where we were plagued by nocuous effects and then moved on
toward a dominant object. The gibbous moon
reminded him of a sad death before moving on toward planets
realized some twenty degrees high in the west. Wait
till the month of July. Slapped by a funeral
the reeds dead branches and watchful rodents
remained in the sky an entire evening as serious
snarls shrieked with amazement. Somewhat concrete proof
that you won't be disappointed at all. Above all
each ponderous birth advanced from the general area
of intercepted particles. What objection do you raise?
The choruses were willing and complete hours before
the imminent plan was announced. It failed to make
a correct approach. As large as it might have been
it was no more earnest than pleasurable childlike
instructions. Spilling out of their eyes they flew away.
They were never seen again. It is not possible. Be cheerful.
The current and coming crisis was informationally aggressive
toward the biology of entropy. Green water urged syllables.
It had abandoned its plan to end its decision
to build money and mercy. On the ground of honor
it was a region of wooded slopes in an endless pursuit
though some kind of lunatic thinks it's OK. Common sense
is quite consistent with the elements they adduce
which decreases their joy in clear sentences and handsome horses.
A glittering silver plan was beside the rowdy train
of history dilating pupils and recovering true goals
unnoticed in a cold blue brook. So I wrote down four
airs for fair and radiant maidens born to come again
and still hard to find. The same ones that wiped us out
disclosed sensible frustration examined or pursued.

Could you have been bewitched? They correlate with actions
forever. Could you gratify obedience? No different than
what you're wondering about in the form of lumps all of me
is comprised of gaping mud. One of the first things was an
  instrument
for sleep. What happens when glimmers feel they should
get together? Thinking spreads beyond foreknowledge of
  extension.
They had been involved in ponderous thought and native water
typical of complete sounds. Loops learn where to survive. They
  approach
admiration obliquely. Tenderness establishes a delegation
thinking every thought rising after a scanty breakfast. Ousted
he pushed good humor and was appallingly deserved. Slices
of heavy appetites went to grievous lengths. We're really in it.
Especially in consideration of things happening in the other
  heart
you are now ready. It is a good rainbow. Interdependence
in an unharvested sea is ancient and stale. It fits too well.
This example brings us softly together as we were in this case
after long being objects of scrutiny. We couldn't joke about that.
We rolled pies and sat down heavily when they blanched visibly
at civilized experience. But now time is described. Otherwise
they'd have learned to see before research was completed. Entities
of a mystical bent are recorded in the deepest decline. Osiers are
  lost
and this is safe. Subsequently sleep spread locally. Today
importance was invasive and grabbed the jagged edges
of basically ungentle adjustments. In mountainous regions
they acquire carbon copies of dead blanks and authentic wild
systems translated into habitual voices and quiet devices
supplied with perpetual revisions urban elements integrate.
        Major functions
are currently being completed. Dwarfing anything previously
imagined their immediate and practical effect is a clear
and present danger. At certain times of day they defend the vice
  with vigor.

An extremely large matrix of equipment is only the tip of the
    iceberg
in the workplace. Only four states require piles of envelopes.
Facades allow corporate tape recorders to open hearts
at moments when glass cases grow boyhoods. Starving
variants found solutions in the snow buried betrayed
and exercising caution under a vital burden vague
and unsatisfied. Mental mouths agreed. With some
green flowers we wait amid paint and insecurity. We tingle
when things are done three times. Politely expressing antipathy
blankets discern processes. That's no good. A tense armor was
    brilliant
in a duality wrong side up. Monkeys unlock cruel doors. That
    noise
must frankly be admitted. Where to start senses birth.
Hours brought memories of concrete answers in prouder
    moments
essential to kisses. I regard the prospect of being spied on
as an opportunity to teach. You can't beat us with wires. A clear
mental state is frozen hard as a mattress. It's time now. Love
shouts in my ears where darkness and daylight touch and never
    return.
Rigid memories are finer than fixed postures. Red cedars
escape overnight. Morons mass near a memorandum.
Thousands taste bread and few describe procedures.
Isolating encrypted messages are only conditional targets and
    vice
versa. From plump individuals really severe dreaming is guided
unknowingly to the pavement by any means possible. We have
to prevent silent days. Primitive fathers are experienced as
    reminders.
And any divergence is due to a temporary confusion. Notice the
    cold lake
dropped shouting into the middle of an arctic waste. How
might that aid us? Hold on. It doesn't matter. We're prepared
sweet dark and intelligent. In a background where meanings are
    assured

monotonous platitudes become denizens of windless
    connotations.
Let's not be so fascinated with all those remote us's. Their way
is offered a third time. Nearer the end the city was preferable.
The phonograph was less mathematical than their tourmaline
    kingdoms.
Their enormous sentences were separate from teeth. Mental
    nature
was less annoying than intelligible benefits sparkling with
judgement. What palpitations were present! White senses rumble
in inexpressible leisure. Don't tell me about it. Injury is heartfelt
and radiant with vexation. Conscious pillows are disinclined
and new noises arise on bored ships stretching toward less
    dangerous spheres.
You know where they are and see their sinister vinegar smiling
    dully.
Winter's privacy is less ravenous. Would you dare to look beyond
that smooth daylight? Waddling overhead she heard his childish
laughter. Genius plundered willing sarcasm more whims
    overlooked
when tedious outsiders felt too free to be reminded of translation.
Variations of twangs forced medication. Cellular accidentals
induced benediction. I'd never have believed it. In two or three
months the manacles could not have been forgotten. Too much
    light.

22 April 1983
New York

Measures

Immoderate use turns to restraint
the foppery of freedom and the morality of prison
unhappily even so surely for a name
as for a prone and speechless dialect.

The aims and ends of burning youth become
more mocked than feared. What seemers seem to be
will soon be seen by those who know the very nerves
of state. All hope is gone: our doubts are traitors.

I'll see what I can do. 'Tis one thing to be tempted,
another thing to fall, for that's the utmost
of this pilgrimage. Did I complain, who
would believe? The prompture of the blood.

Servile to all the skiey influences nursed by baseness
though all the world's vastidity you had, a remedy
presents itself. The place may have all shadow
and silence in it, the time answer to convenience.

It was a mad fantastical trick and severity must cure it.
When he makes water his urine is congealed ice
advised for the entertainment of death. Much upon this riddle
runs the wisdom of this world, no sinister measure.

Unpregnant and dull to all proceedings, we would
and we would not. Forerunning more requital
against the tooth of time and rasure of oblivion,
cut off by course of justice, most truly will I speak.

Be an archvillain with such a dependency
of thing on thing as the warrant's for yourself.
After much debatement in hateful practice without blemishes
someone hath set you on against our substitute.

Give us some seats! Now will I unmask.
In her imagined person and words from breath
as strongly as words can make up vows as instruments
of some more mightier member, he hath set them on.

Did I not pluck thee by the nose for thy speeches?
No longer session hold upon my shame. Thoughts are no
subjects—intents but merely thoughts. Thou art said
to have a stubborn soul, a quickening in his eye.

23 April 1983
New York

HANNAH WEINER

from *Spoke*

AUG 15

what if the   september   flowers hurt   I was prepared

for a great big fall on the WRIST stairs   and I could've

broken my wrist fallen down the stairs   but I was upset

took precautions and slide down easily   and DONT BROKE
                                         YOUR ARM

it absolutely helps to be   selfish entirely for one day

affair in a year Hannah   I think   I was drunken to SHOW

MOTHER on purposely that I drinks BELATED   Aug 31 is on
                                          BIRTHDAY

a monday night WHICH ISN'T HER BIRTHDAY EITHER

I was drunken also walking and his PERIOD   is continuing the
                              PROBLEM
                              IS SOLVED
sentence   work is done   w Indians   imperative

to our affair cultural WORK IS DONE WITH THE INDIANS

ISNT UNTILS IM DEAD because of the spiritual side SAME
                              ·   EXCUSE
                                          ALWAYS
of the praise   they were always indent of   a spiritual

VERY SIMPLE hierarchy ISNT ON THE LINE and we dont

comfort who tells with some leaders it
                              I WAS IT
I was some comfort to the sentence the way out west boy laughs

praise   hierarchical comfort is in the tub where the back
scrub is on the line   sis she pretends she isnt getting older
but I love her the most on thisend page ofthe political brochure
and political brochure ofthisend page atthisend page
but I love her

　　　　　　THE MOST underline of all the parents
in the world   sunshine is our Wednesday night and the
comfort comes unbeliev able ly comfort in $third$ praise in
those help in the whiskey style   I was a robberer once   at
the distinguished clientele   of the rubber boots   and some
celibacy incl included plus dot period plus $saming$ period

someone gets the hint to calm down getting Richard's letter
published was a great big hit   I mean only clairvoyant
material for THE NEXT FOUR YEARS ONLY AND THENS I
QUIT WRITING $forever$ which I dont believe

　　　　　　　LISTEN

sis its ok but dont write the material first and holden
unto your style for the bedroom slippers   we are pleased
we are infinite   but sirname is patience   itself   for
our publishing process   who is calm and rests immed iate ly
or immediately on the current signal on or across the page
is this secret lover or immediate on the falm we are incorrect
spelling on the farm   which is the calm on the farm   or

Reagan distrust newspaper   I am always playing ver carefully
                distribution
                    incl
it said safe   untils I die with only four books

this is included and count journal clair one   and this is

it to me   I am rewriting the prose style   only four books

to be included on the list of the same style per iod same

style on the period same style   or forever we constant

Indians who is living   I am included among the teachers

great of the living style   of the living style comple te

complete of the living style c_ompl_et_e on the same page finish

this wor section these words are inflicted upon by us who

writes in the uneven indent which   I was prepared to fight
                signifies
                    us
for a long time in the indent field   where   it is indent

only   is indented here on the   left hand   margin over the
style
drunken page   which is sacred is the only indent field
                writing
sacred or the Indians

    push it over   on the next line incl   on the next line

included was said it   was   said   it   on the very same line

on the same very line   I was embarras   because of the
                                    QUANTUM

joining principle   of the physics undercover   UNDER COVER

spelled correct underwear   I was visiting   my   mother   last

spring true in the Providence   unusual home   on the paid
                                        sits

I undercover agent   on the Bill   on the two weeks Bill

same name Means   inclu ded   included   on the   Douglas
                                                  Messerli

makeshift plan   I was included on the shit list two drinks

too   included   I ams drunken writing

                                        ON THE MEANS

on the brothers in the verse old style on the verse plan
                          technique
we reverse this is sits twelfth night alone with mother then

we rejoice make it a big master's story return on the January

1st inclusive walking in the somewhere street until November

on the almost myname Im very scared if the Indians follow

me with a truck about   about the   streets   in the
                                                 seen
                                some boys group
of the plural capacity   of the
       government went wild

brain wild   in the submit in the basement store in the

included list   in   the   included   list over on the

cigarette   left   sis its ok to quit and leave the page

finished until Mon night or the allcover rain is coming

down Tues fast or the   believable wearing of the socks

of this page first overtheleft of this believing ofthe socks

which I bought Hannah very careful yesterday   of the

yesterday early
           socks   information in the letter style andquote

of the submissive   pink   slippers   and white tread of

the two weeks bicycle left   rain comes tues and page

completed   the diet completed of the yesterday fun   it is

safe and final   step   on the drinking one glass liquor

of the safetest tread   I was hysterical   YOU POOR DEAR

IT WAS ALL hiera$_{r_{ch}}$ written   down   before   you   Phil Glass

were born uneven
           the last
           line page   and scribbles sheet on the   leftyesterday

sis its a great big quarrel over the publishing procedure

on the page inst   or the page included or the dots Aug 17

either   or the dots either complete   or the dots either

Thurs complete incl   wash the slippers and dont

get y$_{o_{u}}$$_{r}$ mother   drunk or either please we quit   oh someday

quit and takes a chance to calm every$_{b_{o_{d}}}$$_{y}$ down   everybody

down incl   incl history   and dots . . . I saw it this day

slash night slash / on the Indians title of the book wrong

wrong title of the Indian left   on this page incl   included

on this left page which is ferry included Sat on the please

quit 11th period and some dots incl   or forcing extra pages

of the meat mackers or page included inst or my question

period very hard
           deposit   on this third week of my jail
                                          AIR MAIL
sentence   I also sent by air mail a letter to my husband

incl a postage stamp and the enclosed letter incl   included

on the same train   I came in benefit of the words   which

I write more slowly now   much neater and less confusion$_{too}$

under the line is offset and the printers ink is alway

accessible to the modern mind which is alchemy itself

on the page itself   I am very patient reading as the know

it alls line is sometimes very early and the printed line

is accessible to me only through meditation technique

like the grand ol style included oh the   Wed night   I
                              girls Roscant
must see her ver early and spell whoname quiet on the

lonesome night put it in the bard right and the lonesome

night is fire alarm screaming at the night is put it off

the fight   I meant light on the right   side   of the

night   instead of the night   instead   by the bright of

the bright lamp by the bedside by the switch   alone   off

SUSAN HOWE

from *Pythagorean Silence*

we that were wood
when that a wide wood was

In a physical Universe playing with

words

Bark be my limbs my hair be leaf
Bride be my bow my lyre my quiver

1.

age of earth and us all chattering

a sentence   or character
suddenly

steps out to seek for truth   fails
falls

into a stream of ink   Sequence
trails off

must go on

waving fables and faces   War
doings of the war

manoeuvering between points
between

any two points   which is
what we want   (issues at stake)

bearings and so

holes in a cloud   are minutes passing
which is

which
view   odds of images swept rag-tag

silver and grey
epitomes

seconds   forgeries engender
(are blue)   or blacker

flocks of words flying together   tense
as an order

cast off to crows

3.

earliest before sunrise   Last
before sunset

twilight   (between day
and dark)

is about to begin   And with time
I could do it

ends childhood
Time an old bald thing   a servant

(Do this

or that) Time's theme
And so we go on through the deeps of

childhood (afterglow of light on trees)
Daybreak

by dying
has been revealed   Midday or morrow

move motherless

(Oh women women look) how my words
flow out

kindling and stumbling   Sunwise
with swords and heys

a dance of disguise
where breath most breathes   (Books

blaze up
my room is bright) World I have made

empty edge
Father's house forever falling

Catch and sketch the chilly evening

14.

Dream of wandering in woods with

my father
Leaves are white   his dress

is white
(considered as white)

cut as if carved in marble   Pure
outline of form

fading from color and from frame

We look into distance as a dream
What we are

and we are not   Threading mazes

of unwearied thought

Long long years
grain sprouting from body   wheat

and barley

A border-rider's kingdom
(holy horse not to be ridden

holy places not to be trodden) Wheel

of Destiny
Plato's spindle of necessity

pantheon of history shivered into

ruin
Walking about at a gate with keys

Singing the keys

Looking west with a low sun
Mystical gaiety

irrational dimensions of an infinite city

from *Defenestration of Prague*

from Speeches at the Barriers

2.

Right or ruth
rent

to the winds shall be thrown

words being wind or web

What (pine-cone wheat-ear
sea-shell) what

volumes of secrets to teach
Socrates

Banks of wild bees in story
sing in no wood so on

cornstalk and cornsheaf

prodigal benevolence
wealth washed up by the sea

What I find
signal seen by my eye

This winter falls froward
forever

sound and suggestion speared
open

Free will in blind duel

sees in secret houses in sand

each day's last purpose
each day's firm progress

schoolgirls sleeping
schoolboys sleeping and stemmed

I will dream you
Draw you

dawn and horses of the sun
dawn galloped in greek before flame

fugitive dialogue of masterwork

5.

Torn away from number weight

and measure
Ten adventures here forgotten

never touching

To go forward downward
Search for the dead

Benevolent woods and glades
hamadryads

plots and old-plays

A fictive realm
Words and meaning meet in

feigning

without a text and running from
true-seeming

Florimell flees away into the forest

Hide her there
an illusion (fiction)

Beauty of the world
becoming part of the forest

and the reeds
(thousands of years)   Night

monadical and anti-intellectual

no clock running
no clock in the forest

evanishing of the actors into

one another
Am in a simple allegory

Reaching out alone in words oh

peerless poesy

from *The Liberties*

from White Foolscap/Book of Cordelia

children of Lir
        lear

                        whistling would in air ha
                nameless appear—
                Can you not see
            arme armes
                give tongue
are you silent o my swift
                        all coherence gone?
            Thrift thrift
we are left darkling
                waiting in the wings again
thral in the heart of Hell.
            have forgotten—
            must go back—
            so far—
            almost there—
                        vagueness of the scene
where action takes place
                who swiftly
                        apparently real
shoot downward
                Behold
                    is *is*
                    you see
he brought her down.

Startled tourists sleep one hundred years
bird migration, story migration
light snow falling.
Once in awhile some tall tale crops up
great Fairly, little Fairly, liar Liar
and lucky Luck.
But crucial words outside the book
those words are bullets.
Lodged in the ebbing actual
women in the flight of time stand framed.
Rat-roofed caution of a cautionary tale
swallows the rat, a pin, wheat
while singing birds recover lost children.
I am looking for lucky Luck
I am his mother
The moneyed class are lions, wolves, bears
their gems and golden collars shine through the snow.

Running rings
of light
we'll hunt
the wren
calling to a catch of thorn
crying to announce a want
along a bank
carried her child
hovered among the ruins
of the game
when the Queen spins
round
Once again
we'll hunt the wren
says Richard to Robin
we'll hunt the wren
says everyone.

I can re

trac

my steps

Iwho

crawl

between thwarts

Do not come down the ladder

ifor I

haveaten

it a

way

CLARK COOLIDGE

The Death of Floyd Collins

1.

these were contemporaries of the mammoth
looking back up the ridge
on this unfortunate friday morning Floyd
whose stem, extending
no foundation for assuming
sleeps when his temperature is lowest

came upon our first Typhlotriton
gills disappeared and henceforth respiration
any one of which might be the one
to create mystical ideas in the minds
sliding thru their tank
before it ended in a blank wall

because beneath the guano are numerous
time a train rumbled by a whole
to move his powerful leg the rock
led me down a long wooden black space
the north, south, & west surfaces also bore
inch long bugs closely related

2.

neighbors never forgot the cure speleologists do
in a lifetime, he usually he explored alone, with sight
of a boy tramping over cornfields in the middle of winter

he was a stocky boy who would lie down on the thin
mantle of snow & blow into man, muscular
with powerful arms

He spoke little & seldom a breathing hole
in any sense of the word cold air in summer &
warm air in winter, & at other times night, caves
little concerned him, except as it might hold a
suck in air, just as mysteriously

How baked beans in his pocket—knew risks,
for he had several brushes
a cave was further from home, woods, & the words with death
He-came was a cave, & Floyd knew it

"I'd rather be dead, than down past his head"

from *The Maintains*

a nouner
that then again
a mile or such
a maybe moo which say sand's off the so
maybe town down
which as to look about as poses its fuse
a main shines about which ton frowns
this maybe yet even a then hence
its so even pieces
that other such even as one closes
on or in the next over which one's even like
and has one this is

deals much down that say means
say yet again this though
a stowed more since as the tonic seats this tense
through this hence more moo
it is
no
such
as no one
has one

says so as so such's through
as rose a more and then this look to flow done
through over which clear as move
such as whole about
such as it came
left like to that cross that side as like side
such that said so what's even that
is through in it
such loss most likelihood used
as if piece much
off as if out in
one such which thing of tin due
leans that such as one stirs likes
sinks hence the done said of a roof
that's what often meant among meant said part done

might that this which is so mean so to say as even since this's
though's so and might such since the more the more
from stop either also done and that even about such
to current plants it might one is yet
very such small
the very so
such a such
lasts even or as means are about the so
said so to say mingles means and maybes

the such's part close type part the as yet grain one
yet is more close to such's since a means a like having
a sure so and such an even ever through
a yet even too over part of an even said so through
so's just about then one more once this

Fed Drapes

FELL FAR BUT THE BARN (came) up & smacked me
Who're you, bleedin? Fled.
Blat in back of a Victrola Car
is so red is such that sun
fell in the rushes & pen bear appear

the white wrong numeral on the wall
can't take it off with the clock
             down with the clock it . . .
          way
on the board-couch with brass, kindergarten clench joints
backed violet rip into the gas valve
it hemmed & snowed

      the wrong way
         remnant face
           rubber
      the pucker

Thin Places

As if the sun were winding round a spool, this
blaze and shutter, the thread of occultation.
Thus, the swimming tenseness to arrive at surprise.

The shadow of a man, arrow of an avenue otherwise
cheerily null. Bark of a dog chopped to
rhythm in spots. Angle edge, ankle to a brass rod,
whitewash light as elder nod. No one as nothing
in motion but in interval. Signs press as gates
in rattle of their means. A game of link-board
under the streaming dare. Shots, but no pennies
to declare them fallen. The port unravels the
strands, and not an arcade missed, as porcelain
proves porous to the clockwork stain. I make
a life here, I cast. I shut a brain here,
increase the paleness of the melting lens.

Manlius to Coeymans

But could it come up into a limestone so correct, teeth
would be slim by comparison. Have to go under the waterfall
for health and a mouth to pour. White powder pile could be
of snow or rock in flake. Seeds that hold all lime in ledge
to grasp.

Step over on that rock while I picture the edge.
Click of brachiopods, passing on by. Tin can candle in
a pottery hole. Asleep in a slot of two feet, pressing.
An angle that's a cleft that's a move, sky slice opening.
Two hands, two feet, a face. You tell me.

Piling up a ladder to down the scree. Meeting a ledge at
the grass. Dipping metal in water, dumb tone. Rain is ice
to a rock.

Nobody's pine. It sounded odd, that it couldn't be seen.
Not a fit time, glancing the rock for. Position, grain
revision.

A copper center to a grey old hill. Dome airs its load.
Viability placenta. Stairs to the Inn via Nose. Come to.
Lime cave rich in ribs. Nodes of excorial abutment.
And you freeze. Then you twirl your knees. Whole mine
in pockets.

The car to a limestone. Pinning eats in cracks. Tub
lined in dripstone. String them to see it. Climb the ladder
to ring your gong. Assent to a flash, and the smoke that
mutes it. Jams it goes. Type up the shells that complete it.
Enter a stone for some air.

And I've sighted the rock I've seen to its remaining.
Active verb, stone, sense against. A pond in a tree.

Album—A Runthru

I look in that one kind of dwindled. And in this,
look up, a truncheon in my fist, tin pot
on my head, the war. My father, I'm looking at, is my
age then and thin, his pants streak to the ground,
shadows of rosevines. . . His father sits beneath
a cat. Here the shadow has more flavor than my
trains, elbow on livingroom floor, bangs that
curl, opera broadcast, The Surreptitious Adventures of
Nightstick. I lie in the wind of the sun and hear
toots and smell aluminium smoke. The tiny oval
of my mother's youth in back and the rest is dark.
Sundays, the floor was black. At the beach, here
I'm a nest of seaweed, an earlier portrait of
surrealists I saw later, a stem of grey what
rises from my scalp. My hair is peaked in brine.
And this here hat, dark green fedora over same green
corduroy suit for a trip to the nation's capitol,

how far askance I've been since and never another
hat. Cromium rods, the hand in the guide's pocket
seems far removed. Blurry shoes on sandstone steps,
double and over exposed. Then in this one the SECRET
points to my head, shaved, and emblem, OPEN, striped
in "pirate" T-shirt and HERE IT IS. My elbow bent,
upright this time, behind a pole. I had yet to
enter at this snap the cavern beneath my sneakers.
To the right my soles protrude from beneath a boulder,
for I had trapped my mother and she asked Why.
Taken. Given. Flashlight brighter than my face,
another grotto, where the ball of twine, indirection,
gave out but we never got very far in, Connecticut.
I swim out of another cave in a further frame, cramped
gaze of sunlit days, apparel forgot. Later I reel
in a yell as my cousin takes a bite from my shank
beneath ranchhouse breezy curtains of Marion. On a trudge up
from the gasoline rockpit in the gaze of Judy Lamb,
she carries my pack, my jeans rolled as I step on
a pipe, Estwing in hand and svelte as only youthful can.
Most of those rocks remain and she married a so-so
clarinetist. My greygreen zipper jacket leans against
a concrete teepee, my father looking bullchested stands
before. Perhaps we had just argued. Central Park cement
steps of pigeons, the snow removed. Overexposed
whiteshirt at the drums, stick fingers ride cymbal
at the camera raised, livingroom Brenton with orange
& black "sea" wallpaper and orange&black tubs. I wore
a wristwatch then and never again, drumtime hitching
me past it. I graduate from highschool in white dinner
jacket and diploma and frown, too many hot shadows
back of the garage. Must roll up the bedroll with
skinny arms and lam for the caves. Dave & A. Bell by
the Ford Country Squire first time allowed alone to tool.
Bleak grass scapes of Knox farm. Rope down a crack,
mosquitoes and Koolade, sun dapple leaf moss sandwiches, ache.

Then in this group more drums on the roof, the gravel
and the flat, a cover attempt for no album even thought.
I tap and step in the dim known street. Lean on a
chimney to inhabit the sky, deep with drops. Here
I'm pressed on a wall of Tennessee limes, stones-throw
from mouth of the underground we camped in. Too many
thoughts, elide. Then lie on a beach in a doughnut
pattern shirt with a stick, a pipe?, in my mouth as my
cousin grins shiny beyond. Truro, also waiting for the
caves. With the poets then I'm fat and the driveway is
dark, the clapboards all white in a day of all talk.
This then all ends in color, my red bandana and shirt out
on Devil's Pulpit, open hand addressed to the grey
where Hawthorne and Melville now view of a highschool.
While the water still spills, and the cat squints at leaves
blown, my father wears Brahms, families lean in on one
for a group shot, and the rock remains shattered in a star.

from *Mine: The One that Enters the Stories*

XVII

Here I will say it, but it keeps leaving me. Here I will parry
with elbow of monk. Here I will return from the moon, but
there's a catch to any catch of light. Holds that revolve 'round the
spineless mind as the straps fall from the body of dreams nights.
There's a yellow patina on the plastered leg that wasn't shown
before. Liars are we all so bodied to our constituency, of a
reduced gold the moon stained a pillar for our hollowed young
love. And where I had wedgewood it had better said wormwood,
the flavors of a drowntable blackstar abutment on coils of essence
and fingers tapping gall. The Latin is divided on this point.

How to say, wrung of all sky and mean it today on the prisms of inwardness. The boys approach the face of adventure but my words again saddle their stall. I don't know a thing but point. This must be the riddance or the absolute. Why am I shut to the present flavors? The knife calms down between a coin and its absence, that coin being my name and who would flee from it. None but my own. In a word mine my title, all riddance despite? And I see myself step up to that face, so thought as if handle ever gone.

From here on this page the world is unknown. Thus start enumerations of the hidden. Upon the layers of subsequent rock earth and seeds there lies a layer of birds. This data is taken as an active consumption, even of the earlier strata by the capstones of the sentence. To dissimulate is to return, as on the noted planet where at a certain age one turns aside, grows back through youth and finally has to "go back in". The birds have disappeared. Why then is there anything left visible on this descriptive world?

Why stop there? I have an urge to continue each sentence till there's no room for another, then the urge to stillness stops it. So I go my way, by myself. And the windows of the world click and the trees shut. What's name would bear repeating? At such a point words tear my thoughts to such a pretty pass. That Picasso's Egyptian lady covers the Delicate Arch. And my room fossilizes as I watch back to nineteen oh five.

Not to be entirely determined by the recently read. I have seen the cloth that sticks to certain shades of air. Tell the story that has never been thought on before. The one that raises its own hairs, volleys down its own passes. The mouth that opened in the box canyon asking for a halt to pastels. Mesas are a natural for the notion to bore holes in a tube and blow. As the jay hops to the branch, the tree slows down or slows it down. I must have a work where things go.

I drove through this old world this afternoon

and it was ancient, quiet, lean and brass
peach gas in bean stacks, babes on bikes of wood
humans held in shelter of their lives

The earth spread wide in folds beneath the turns
of men though new their stores of use were old
as if nothing had stopped that once had turned to brown
alarms of act all casual seemed a gown

I passed the rows of brick where Easter neared
with eggs of varnished ice that vanished not
in air as blue to touch as mountain's thrust is rough
on windows hard with dust that I had traced there once

The town then filled the notch with laddered woods
and brightness hives of stuff all hands grow bare to touch
in crowds that leaned at noon contrariwise
would knot my route make prisms of my eyes

So casts the light this land no time at all
an eddy of the force to elbow shirts
as far beneath the ledge the needle drops
that banisters protrude from stories fast and small

I smell the fall, I dodge the urge
I whistle through the rates of atoms dear
the sky so clear the land to bulge
mere mention of halt plan a care

The light is over
man a boundless stare

2.

Then stood upon a bench that ruled my car
through venturesome whole days far by all unmarked
and watched the boardsides strand an ankled past
by turbines locked by keys of empty glass

As home absorbs the time that held it up
I fill to amber with the light of days
held waste till afternoon had turned them up
and held my mind in furnish of their state

Whole hills of housing edges fold
then massed will each thing fully last
and time come to boil the each turn dark
that breath will cool to beads upon a mast

And as I pass to catch the lost anew
is praps to spy the end of things ahead
and none more bogus than the thing that's new
that fades into a background still more fast

The old ones state their case as plain as sum
I leave them there as thought of one day done

LYN HEJINIAN

from *Writing Is an Aid to Memory*

28.

we are parting with description
termed blue may be perfectly blue
goats do have damp noses
that test and now I dine drinking with
others
adult blue butterfly for a swim with cheerful birds
I suppose we hear a muddle of rhythms in water
bond vegetables binder thereof for thread
and no crisp fogs
spice quilt mix
know shipping pivot
sprinkle with a little melody
nor blot past this dot mix
now for a bit and fog of bath rain
do dot goats
swift whipper of rice
a type as cream
into a froth
ranking a time when rain looms
I part the swim and width whereas
hob for swing yard note
product in the woody weeds
trees in the foreshortening

a source "draws" shortening
  by an inkspot over the four rivers
    darkness ficing no flaw pink
                the stain whose at him stuff suggested
      is visible as follows (cone in space)
          old waters
              this morning over fringed crop involving
          quantity
    it lasts into the empty sky shopping and glittering
    I can picture the marked page
        poke beauty
            sunset like a pack of dogs
            swaying with daylight
    it is late afternoon and I hurry
        my fault of comfort
              the streets of traffic are a great success

from *My Life*

Like plump birds along the shore Summers were spent in a fog that rains. I had claimed the radio nights for my own. There were more storytellers than there were stories, so that everyone in the family had a version of history and it was impossible to get close to the original, or to know "what really happened." The pair of ancient, stunted apricot trees yielded ancient, stunted apricots. What was the meaning hung from that depend. The sweet aftertaste of artichokes. Even a minor misadventure, a bumped fender or a newsstand without newspapers, can "ruin the entire day," but a child cries and laughs. They had ruined the Danish pastry by frosting it with whipped butter. It was simply a tunnel, a very short one. Now I remember worrying about lockjaw. The cattle were beginning to move across the field pulled by the sun, which proved them to be milk cows. There is so little public beauty. I found myself dependent on a pause, a rose, something on paper. It is a way of saying, I want you, too, to have this experience, so that we are more alike, so that we are closer, bound together, sharing a point of view—so that we are "coming from the same place." It is possible to be homesick in one's own neighborhood. Afraid of the bears. A string of eucalyptus pods was hung by the window to discourage flies. So much of "the way things were" was the same from one day to the next, or from one occasion (Christmas, for example, or July 4) to the next, that I can speak now of how we "always" had dinner, all of us sitting at our usual places in front of the place mats of woven straw, eating the salad first, with cottage cheese, which my father always referred to as "cottage fromage," that being one of many little jokes with which he expressed his happiness at home. Twice he broke his baby toe, stubbing it at night. As for we who "love to be astonished," my heart beats shook the bed. In any case, I wanted to be both the farmer and his horse when I was a child, and I tossed my head and stamped with one foot as if I were pawing the ground before a long gallop. Across the school playground, an outing, a field trip, passes in ragged order over the lines which mark the hopscotch patch. It made for a sort of family mythology. The heroes kept clean, chasing dusty rustlers, tonguing the air. They spent the afternoon building a dam across the gutter. There was too much carpeting in the house, but the windows upstairs were left open except on the very coldest or wettest of days. It was there that she met the astonishing figure of herself when young. Wherever I might find them, however unsuitable, I made them useful by a simple shift. The obvious analogy is with music. Did you mean gutter or guitar. Like cabbage or collage. The book was a sort of protection because it had a better plot. If any can be spared from the garden. They hoped it would rain before somebody parked beside that section of the curb. The fuchsia is a plant much like a person, happy in the out-of-doors in the same sun and breeze that is most comfortable to a person sitting nearby. We had to wash the windows in order to see them. Supper was a different meal from dinner.

If there's nothing out the windows look at books

Hold back, as less from friends; hold the book, hold up, then hold on tight, hang on. Strawberries fortynine. A man on the street swings his arm out to get a look at his watch, stretching to get his wrist out of the suit jacket, two on the watch. A translator must try to keep all of the most interesting words. Is it a pattern that we see or only a random placement of the stupid little tiles. Or a place by water in early spring. This stop and start is bumper to bumper. We sat in a bar and Charles recited a poem by Emily Dickinson which "made her come alive." There's plenty to express a color in the paper. He marched around the basement for about 10 minutes, playing his line. When feeling nothing again, said to be happy, having nothing but fun. The park was crammed, more of an adventure for the dog. A natural climber, a goat, got to the top, the way a bird gets to the end of the limb, or a timber top, as it should be rather than could be. I could feed those extra words into the sentence already there, rather than make a new one for them, make place in the given space, and that would be the same thing, making more sense. Such displacements alter illusions, which is all-to-the-good. Such diction is used in discourse to put it possibly. Yet better left unsaid if I could have. A pause, a rose, something on paper. Waiting for sleep, sleep waits. The burglar had come back a second time, but this time the dog was ready. She is slow except expects to bark. Such charged habit is tradition. There is no "sameness" of the sky. Things are settled before we go, as I've got my own to do. That isn't the dog barking that's the dog guarding the house, a cave, and we've retreated into it. When I ran out of seeds the birds ran from me. In the dark twilight, so upright, uneasy, the sunset offshore was buried alive. I never swept the sand from where I was going to sit down. Was also a friend, one point breaking close. The postman became a mailman. Moving to some harder way to see without blocking what's to see. Top time—with a finger and a stretch of smooth sand. Dust is hairy dirt, furry dirt. I laugh as if my pots were clean, in good spirits, well-rested, humming a nameless, a tuneless, tune. The degree to which you're sucked in, you soak it up. One looks out windows at windows, nose in a book. One of my favorite words was bird and will be.

from *Redo*

13. Determinism

Putting facts by the thousands
into the world, the toes take off
with an appealing squeak which the thumping heel
follows confidentially, the way men greet men.
Sometimes walking is just such elated

pumping. As the dog bumps
its head, the fog clears
and it's sunny for the Sonnet
Scouts march to (I was humming
to myself but making the sound

in my head, not my neck
where it remained, resonating against my temples)
all the elements of which count: wordlessly-
wars, prank-youth, heavily-all-together.
They flicker, in order fully to correspond

with the perceptibility of life.
Unfortunately this is a very busy time
in which too much is noticeable. As news
fills the sheets, topical blooms
fill the streets and slope

against the coast. People
think I have written an autobiography
but my candor is false (I hear a few shots
slouching at my realism).
As if corralled, or slowed by cold

all that intentional and unintentional experience
is unable to stop or change. Restlessly
I moved to new positions—spots
and postures—that's all. I am myopic
with determination. And so

just as one might run one's fingers around
the edge of a glass
to make it squeal, similarly
in the hollow night a car circles
the edges of my consciousness

and this sentence is emitted.
But of course occasionally one sinks
into the sand that fills the locale
with its clean opinionless lingering.
The sea is being swept off

near the sea front. Every dime
is a meter piece. The shore
is very thin. Days
wash past at their normal level
wherever the shadows break.

from *The Guard*

8.

The bottled message is twisted in the bottle
black with life. I
am indeed no longer a beginner who throws herself
on such dense inverted picturing—I too have discarded

and discarded. My aporia achieved
the glamorous anticipation of an answer.
As birds enter bristling

with the melodic excitement of wind on the spines
of a rough nest. Who refuse
to extrapolate a law of gravity
from anything that falls. "Heaven"
takes its place in nature as a hoop, a tongue
and a tooth. The bucket
is a utensil for mulish continuing.

Some hormones repeat, some are senses
of humor. The thump of apples falling
with noble aim. A mouthful of lawn.
And I hurried to get in every projection.
Undivided literature. Noted the murmurous
monotonous sound effects
"drip-drip-splashing-drip-

splash-dripping, splash-splash
drop drip drop
drip" which we have set out
to receive it. Confiding
in this aquarium . . . the knowledge of "empty"
surpasses the capacities of language . . .
the swivel, a mound . . .
"I am a construction worker, I work at home"
with stiff serenity . . . this
is the difference between language and "paradise"

from *The Person*

X.

A person is clinging
with the monotony of generosity
I always dream when I understand
that sentence in a sense-impression
Jealousy of perception is a grammar
The appearance of the person in nature

I don't want to be an active child
a corpse with impartial drives
an avenue along the floor
to say that "I invented
tortures"
the pink distribution
Fat, terrible vulnerability
of the neck (milk
is a word for it)
A sentiment should not have a noun
It's ALL "person"

With kissing you suck
all music
Your cheek is only like
your other cheek
Well, sing it
and you will see that it takes the repetition
to give it its great strength
And imagine it
backward: oh! that's too much!
Paradise & paragraphs
They can be indifferent
under the pink skin of distribution
Sincerity is an intestinal part

"I am becoming an unmuffled condition"
of differences
A river between two loaves
Admire! a condition of limbs
in various combinations of consciousness
I used once to suppress this . . . this personality event
I'll say what I do
without faith inflamed
or the vivid imagination of its failing
in a sense-impression

A portrait—do the body
with food, physique, and action—
as in involuntary eating
I'm baffled by the psychology
of my characters—it unrolls
with the monotony of jealousy
Freedom in strangeness
Disaster in sleep
Entertainment in poetry
The person has monstrous ears

TED GREENWALD

Privets Come into Season at High Tide

Privets come into season at high tide.
The night on the Great Neck side
near Steppingstone the bargeman walks
over the water the refrigerator opened the mailman fell out.
Opening the closet the grocery boy fell out
banging his head on the floor his knee.
The snow bushes 40 years preparing dinner,
or the laugh on the rug, gold threads weaving in
& out over the bodies on the floor.
First sack, the corrugated box lit up
under the lawn lamp the rippled footsteps
running from the scene of the hiding, tumbled out on-
to the floor.   "What are you doing in there?"
"I am searching.   It is good to be free again."

The first race we took a beating
lurching free from the vain control of sense.
As your hair goes so
goes the subtle undercurrents passing thru the foot in-
to the chin, & up.   Even if you ground
yourself with the closet door the tension
is mixed, the filth of corners have no effect
& proselytic airs the room have no effect.
The hum.   The prop limbs stacked in the corner
penetrate handle & space between finger-
tip plastered the original conviction.

Dialogue:
white hair melting in the warm air
rising from the radiator in the corner, the whiteness.
The hand.   The space between fingers.
Walking slowly on the rocks.

Character:
nubile
syrup the syrup
marrow from the lips of well
the spray, the seaweed, her grass side,
sweating with a light touch on the neck,
walking the ghastly hours deliveries are made;
dotted hours, & the rabid denture chewing the long gloss.

Her maple thigh—mole . . . cheek—
the chattering of teeth on the ground,
count out plums & grapes
leading the eyelid bay & stars.   The line.
The whim drawing the danger thru the dust out of the corner.
The underbrush kelp.   Transforming the hedge circuits.

Lies

only
avenue
of
escape

just
around
the
corner

And, Hinges

Fog hanged over the park, the night cold, and, clean
against the tree you leaned in the sunlight, breathing
he spinned the car out on fine gravel near the gate
she laughing at the tree   standing straggly   over the fence.

And, the drain clogs, when I shower, with my hair,
queasily, paper rolling out of your handbag, glinting sequins,
and, she stood, laughing   over her shoulder   by the spinning
    wheels
"how do you get to the station, from here?"

Skin   smelling clean, after the shower, and, dark,
merrily, tempting   me to talk to you, and, asking if you've
    seen,
and, turning to her friend, tall, and, skinny next to her,
"Taking the first   turning you come to   in the book, and
    curve

round it."   Warm moisture rising, I rise sluggishly,
the latest news from Paris, tho I've never been there, calm
"he never could control the damn thing, and, thinks he's
    Fangio."
She knew better than to laugh, but she did   anyway
    ,laughing

hide behind a tree, and, light bark late, keeping the neighbors
    late,
and, you ask me "have you seen the latest news from Paris?"
Out back someone   mugging laughter   ,and, he thought over
    the problem
to bust her gut.   "Did you see that turning   the horse
    made dog?"

Hours arranged handily on the wrist, I scrutinize them,
and, and tell you "I've never been there myself, have you?"
How to get back on the road, and, keeping his hands intact.
"Absolutely splendor, the light on   shimmering her hand."

Hourly, and, after dinner they scrutinize me.   "How we love,"
and, you answer, "yes, dozens of times."   I look at my watch
He's such a bore.   Always running around fast over the
    place."
She knew better than to know   know better than his local
    hands, placed

filling mail order slips, out, sleeping afterward   in the down,
and, you shiver, and, laugh, "it's really terrible what's happen-
    ing!"
how it sounds in reverse.   Scared, and, the hairs turning
    prematurely
gray, respectably, over the nearest sand mound in the pile

pillow I puff up with my hand   before the light   goes out
"oh yes, I agree, would you care to join me for lunch,"
spun gravel rising under the wheels, and, him sitting.   The
    clay lump
she picked up some too, running it thru   her veiled fingers

in the fireplace.   And, you say "you are thirsty," and, I
    believe,
and, you take my hand, handily switching your pursing lips
to the other side clinging higher under the screech, and, wheel.
And, she looked at him, blinking owlly back tears.   And, they

came anyway, you, and, "I am thirsty too, for more dinner wine"
"not having any money, but wanting to speak to you so much."
"Who?   Who?   Does he think he is?   Anyway?"
She knew there was nothing to do but curve out the light ground

under her, and several more candles to warm the room.   To
the other
side of your mouth.   "That's okay, I love lunch in the park,
anyhow."
His phantom figure stalking shadow after shadow after dark.
And, cry til a little pool formed, and, she rose to go home.

Complete Balancing Weather Meets

Complete balancing weather meets
With the eye of complete off-balance brain
Tottering through verbs
Dew covers the shoe
With minute observations
Piling up in an organic unity life chair and sitter
Dog floats in with pipe slipper and paper
Sits partly over the instep of unshorn foot
Snores like a saw through the glories of news logs
The reader soon falls his head down in bliss
Or is it a sleep without dreams
In a city where the nose
Comes occasionally to a water-smelling patch of haze
On the face
Moving toward the river in a phrase

Lapstrake

The cleat curved you curved the spider
the coil of alcoholic fumes
the webbing of sail & sunset,
over the mountain the distance: Colorado,
New Mexico.   In Tucson
the beggars are gymnasts good riders swaying side-to-side
are fine steerers covering much territory
the backroom towel & soap the front leg.

The drainpipe of your leg the lapstrake side of the shipping
the barge traveling at speeds incredible to the eyes
in the movement of lips carpeting seaweed with
pitch & roll of the movements of your leg,
your lips the errors of your back lingered on your chest
when the spider came to milk the thread of your leg
the bending the back or arch
the cleat punctuating gulls, or blue packet.

Stemming the flow of guitar music
craving the movement of the arm, the total movement,
from the sleep tarantulaic
iodine in the mouth
the leg moving over the hills
the horses frothing at the inn black hairs draping
your breasts with prairie roses, the rope on
the side of the saddle the movement of the cleat tying up the
    ship
side lapstraking the breeze
Juno nibbling at 20th century foliage, the seaweed,
iodine the mouth watering at the sight of the spider,

the hovering movement of the facets
leggings moving up the thighs in a crawl
up the mountains the search for the rope hanging at the saddle

the mounting of the easy charge thru the streets
Cheyenne, Yuma in the afternoon the border the night before
nibbling at the conscientious boundary.
"make good time?"
"more than thrifty miles or the devil's league. the cactus is
    boring."
"are you carrying spare parts of hair?   leg?   or other?"
only several drinks to unparch the deck
the reeking odor of major feet in the mountain,
slicking down package of roots to chase
in the distance lying under a scrub the gray remnants of rug
the gray pellets of shoes & legs
bathing the horses in the pool.

He would never make the border & the meat tasted
fine the fire burning his tongue, trying to relieve
the tension of the first mask, the second
wave of iodine cluttering his tongue,
the web the tastiness of tongue on flesh.

PETER SEATON

Antonville

I provide my past with you, the most
Urgent musical interests offering my writing
The letter in which poetry produces the uses
And enlightenments of the world. I have
In mind a music in which ideas which meet
My progress with an exposé of the principle
Of rendition alter my edge to an understanding
Blow to my proud part. It discusses me
And why and how the most intense
Intention fuses coherence to a string
Unimaginable and purely written. Tonic
Lines teem with bright proportions of how
To say wanting to say my wild stone
Intervals, my naive lookalikes dressed
In the heat of the pen, tuned up
And swallowed up by awe for a throng
Of mortal absolutes, the effects of mass
And its taste, dizzy praise in print
Tearing up the precious pages of my heart's
Histories until the slightest particle subject
To the fatal presentiment begging to be
Imposed on conscious sense unequivocally listens.

Two Words

It's clear, you run wild with my message. All the answers
We got are invoked by human looks
And still shape our mind. By making anticipation
Adorn a local geophysical mind something in these words
That's marked by a pair likes you.
But the new words wouldn't bring you into some colony
Discovering a wider world, spaces of what
The words tell me to discover the hunger of all nations
And resist you by a move in which I would be
Based only on the same continent
Before my appeals are absent from my lies.
In unions quickly concerning you
Bled and present in father's profound books
Or sections you think you're sold
For the possible sign, a nerve
Fabricating the confrontation with a reader I left you
Solving with cultural ease and attributing
Books in which you can have enough of a language to
Small orange and white tones and hesitant slices
Of what that had to be, the house to house world.
Better take charge of the poor poets with feet bare,
Knowledge bare until the spirit in the blood appears
As though I were about to mind the things you dread.

Most specialties soften us for what you call
In America a theme
That at once had occurred to you
Making things change, new things
That begin in the development of peering
At the pillars of idleness. You bet you won't
Dance in my head or in a den of lions
To desert me
Where I structure my certainty
Unsummoned with my lies, in the silence
Of the nights. But it isn't true.

But I don't recall animate beings fitting this rule
To the ideas that you can find. I told Goethe how
After only a few readings there were diagrams
Differentiating groups to talk to. And that
We consist of lifetime or daytime or nightime
Writing to be the one
To endure because the emphasis
Creates a feeling you're in, of some way to fit
Whatever you want to continuous attention
Which would not be character
Enthusiastically flown from your pen.
Between the ancient quantity of each framed verse
I bought a word, both words, that start with size
Function, kind and color, that would look lively to express
Illusion subject to breathing ratios
And emptied of an instant both written and verbal
In which a coyote, a raven or a bear wants
Entire other animals for analogies. It says
A need is everywhere, in lakes, in one
Of nature's longing works and in the craters
On shields and shorelines and in the crater
And mounds of stone cones
And vents kick up again behind roots and cracks and in
Fumes across the deep wild vertebrae
Tan old proverbs. Maybe it's Pinocchio
Recalling implants of intensity
Threatening to boil over with daily
Activity and reluctantly starting to turn out fine
Lines with impurities and flesh over it all.

So it was nice to hear somebody escape
The dreams come true. But since you trust others
To accuse you of how much has been written
To change night into day and into the best example
Of the only thing you know, the center of life today
I'll ask you questions of the most variety
Cover to cover while wondering if

The hitch in the wish turns the pages and
If life sounds simple pulsing with lies based
On writing that supports the body
And clings to it with a pen. I must devote
More and more of you to that
Capacity suffering the statement
Of the greatest wishes amended to writing
This insistence. It's not any other skill.
It's a lie.

The trail to the talking outside things
Colors drum and so forth sticks to petty channels
In the body. You sent me to exhaust objections
To a word fitted for description, to cause this world
That could be you restricted to the field of my example
Because the written thing protects me, defends me
Here and there lacking cross sections
Often found in your room. It's true, two long words
Struck the mind to anticipate the ivory silk bodies
Which thou dearest writes and used to write
Print free peculiarities. You won't get me to say
Parts of my pictures didn't drop out of the blue.
It wasn't that intentional. One can still walk
During a syllable impressing thought
On constituting matter, in advance
Of what a poem really is? Exposing what I love most
To a figure in my life stirs references
To memories, its all real vision ancient
Footprint music made you publish
When we were kids, when the contents originate
The wicked heart which beat in love
With those about to leave.

Who often had to see all lies, all bodies
Reaching for this shock to counter reason
To decide to follow your example keener, more

Demanding, more intense
And expansive and at liberty to see them soon.
I didn't hear talk but there seems to be space
To stop it and all the definite vast horizontality
Keeps going. Only you, the hardiest person
Are unable to reason losing the cataclysm
Affecting your work, rewarding the
Occasional greatest rhythm there
With changes while bare nightmare skies with miles
Of light gives you what you've never heard
Of knowledge of sore red and white discourse
Lasting years and numbering one and you
Don't have to worry about floods or speech or prayer
And do things, do you think that hurt?

MICHAEL PALMER

The Library is Burning

(Eighth Symmetrical Poem)

The library is burning floor by floor
delivering pictures from liquid to sleep

as we roll over thinking to run
A mistaken anticipation has led us here

to calculate the duration of a year
in units of aloe and wood

But there will be no more dust in corners
and no more dogs appearing through dust

to question themselves uncertainly
Should it finally be made clear

that there's no cloud inside no body
no streetlamps, no unfoldings at five o'clock

along the edge of a curved path
Masters of the present tense

greet morning from their cautious beds
while the greater masters of regret

change water into colored glass
The stirrings are the same and different

The stirrings are the same and different
and secretly the same

The fear of winter is the fear of fire
disassembling winter

and that time the message was confused
it felt the most precise

On the Way to Language

The answer was
the sun, the question

of all the fragrances undressed
by the rats in the Pentagon

is Claude's, little
memory jars

empty of their pickled plums
and the tiny

pile of dried bodies under the floorboard
(we had to sell that car)

Summers are always difficult
arriving too soon, too

much wind and the absolute
darkness when it finally descends

over the plantation. We're not ashamed
of our immense wealth

even somewhat proud
of the cleanliness of the servants' quarters

From the sound of their weeping
they seem happy enough

in their work, childlike
and contrite. The answer was

memory, an efficient
engine driven by earthly

remains and the question
of the valley of desire

crossed by the bridge
of frequent sighs

Seven Forbidden Words

"Mon chat sur le carreau cherchant une litière"
Baudelaire, "Spleen"

Who peered from the invisible world
toward a perfectly level field. Terms
will be broken here (have been broken here).
Should a city of blue tile appear
no one will be listening there.
He stood up, walked across the room
and broke his nose against the door.
A was the face of a letter
reflected in the water below.
He watched cross-eyed
learning a few words at a time.
The sun rose behind your shoulder
and told me to act casual
while striking an attitude of studied repose.
You grew these flowers yourself
so how could you forget their names.
The yellow one is said to be uncommon
and the heart tastes as expected, tender
and bitter like an olive
but less violent. It has been summer for a day
or part of a day
with shades drawn. The fires were deliberately set
and the inhabitants welcomed them.

Book of the Yellow Castle

This can be seen as placing a mirror against the page.
The mountain is where we live, a circus there, a triangle
of unequal sides the days no sun appears.

This is life in the square inch field of the square foot house,
a September particle, biochip, or liquid in a jar,
and here is snow for the month to follow, light easy to move

but difficult to fix. The cat on the book has fleas.
It's a real cat with real fleas at least,
while the book is neither fixed nor field.

As soon as you had gone an image formed in order to be erased.
First an entryway then a left and right which seemed to be the
      same.
This letter explains everything and must never be sent.

This other arranges figures along an endless colonnade
imperceptibly darkening toward red. One pretends to be the case
the other is. Mornings the hands tremble, evidence of a missing
      thought.

Arrows will tell you where the words are meant to lead,
from hall to hall apparently. The hair is thinner
and the veins stand out a bit more.

Who could have known he'd be dead within the week,
victim of a loosening thread, the system by which we perceive.
Thus the castle above valley and plain, the logical circuitry and
      other such tricks,

the constant scanning, all kinds of features built in.
And thus the difference between sign and sigh, and the bells
      which signal a return.
The dog instructs the goats, the man instructs the dog.

Should we count the remaining trees to decide what they mean as
    well,
traces of a conversation possibly, or a larger plan. You enter the
    stories as a surd
and sleep through them, ignoring successive warnings,

shards of cloisonné, broken table legs, a canopied bed.
They are there because the rest have left.
These are scalings of a sentence.

Lens

    I failed to draw a map and you followed it perfectly
    because the word for "cannot" inscribes itself here
    to define an atmosphere of absolute trust
    which both fastens and unfastens us.

    The branches of the pine drooped heavily
    in the moist air and this was pleasant
    though at times it felt a little unpleasant
    that he couldn't balance on his head

    where the water trickled down the rocks.
    So everything seemed small, even the problem
    of whether to buy a new car
    or to add a new gadget to the old car

    to maintain pride of place on the block. He appears
    to have seen the black pubic hair and the vagina
    of a woman who squatted there to piss,
    the gypsy nurse perhaps

who dealt in magic
holding the infant up with both hands.
The mist would first blur the forest's outline
then half reveal the huge limbs of the trees

or the bedside clock ticking, a red
and a white rose fastened to her breast.
She had sunk into a corner. He told
how gazing at a mountain pool

had once induced a kind of waking sleep
which led to other things.
("I am the lover in the sense of dust"
were his exact words, spoken softly.)

The child was crying out and bleeding.
Indifferently he moved on—the way
did not matter, up or down,
a few steps should be enough.

Facades for Norma Cole

These ornaments as we pass
to which thin lines are attached
the straight dark hair, bordered

hollows and lights, double spirals
imagined weights of things
If only I could draw, then

there would be an owl here
a fox in the elm's shadow
Bill do you remember the Chinese man in the stained grey over-
        coat

lying dead on the snow
by the brick wall
A remarkable document

which must never be published
He turned round to answer
but she was gone

then ran through the streets before passing out
on the steps of a synagogue
the face no longer recognisable

even to my closest friends
These crystals, however
Or put it this way

the particles circle and circle inside the ring
all the while accelerating
until finally by the billions they collide

That's how the missing one was found
Let's call it W for now
which fuels the stars

and so add one more line
extending from the woman with naked breasts
at the center of the arch

to the cat asleep on the child's bed
They spoke of exactly this over coffee
until the glass door shattered

letting the damp wind enter
In her room she showed me
a photograph of her lover

young, heavily muscled and tanned
from several months at sea
We drank wine, smoked

opium through a glass pipe
and climbed to a place on the ridge
a field of nettles and anise

where the remains of the city could be seen
not this city but a previous one
called the pissing rose

or the rhymesters' rose
or the rose of even numbers
or the rose of indecision

or the rose of precise description
or *la rose dialectique, Dominique*
all yours again

in tenuous modes of oscillation
'neath a vestigial sky
"Look—there was a wall here once"

No one did this
It came about by itself
during yesterday's storm

RAY DI PALMA

The Bed

Dark o'clock
Be solid maybe inside
But adequately
Dead one by the sequence

And tumble
Light
Presses daylight
Brick to waver brick

To build or boundary
You'd think
Come closer
And the voices

All so flat
Half-fallen off
Hunting the careless
In the parade

How can white be
The moon looks down
And turns
Thin and bitter

So I'll go back
We'll reach
Every back and mirror
Turning dangerous

Between the nostrils
Earning a little borrowed air
Right right proportions
Crabbing and opaque between yawns

A first coat a
Second coat or
Are you hearing things
Perfect decoys

Like the tug of yellow
Like neighboring thumb and finger
Yours and hers
Mine and yours or not yours and hers

Delicate and unperturbed
A slithering iridescence
That would be inscrutable
Were it not fact

Wan clever minutely natural
Nearly perfect
Gone to seed like columbine
Nearly perfect

As when all the lights
Go out you can walk backwards
With perfect impunity
And say so

How clever to be invisible
A length of iron pipe in your pocket
Your voice a shadow
Behind your teeth

An inheritor
Pumping the space with decimals
Approach the cultivating claw
Brother

Where four billion years
Of nature two million dollars
One million miles and thirteen
Hours inspire chat

There there now the coincidences
Back to back the convincing quirks
Make for the calmly circumspect
A perfect garden in which to dance

Moves winding meticulous
As buds twist a branch
Light dismantling a wave
Memory copying touch

A surge and violent hush
Composed aurora but can't trust
The wind now though it's a great response
I prefer to the ripeness of words

Passing through a perfect frame
Of backlit steam reds greens blues
Pausing just long enough
To take the measure

The lines the four corners
Embody memory large and impersonal
No better to say
The stiff angles of deflection

No better
To say no better to say
Comes and goes but just so far
Purpling as it happens

Amicably solemn
The remote terrors of proportion
Confide the raw
Dreaming the intricate

Unaccompanied
The word of a stranger
Nostrums and random exceptions
Inclination or opinion

The fastidious analogue
The ballad and the prejudice
Intense solitude
Wilderness to wilderness

The coin or the kindness
A high tambourine
Shrugged shoulders
Spectacle volunteer

Peculiar to certain orders
Like the assassin
Broken imperfectly on a conviction
But enthralled by a mere prospect

Dependable phantoms
The song after the music
Not the chase but
The paint drying

Grammar is black
Syntax is starch
Reverend X
Reverend Y

A thin black line
The collar of the coat turned up
Evertheless I liked the way mere touch
Could make the beads spin

Made me feel tribal
In my secure sense of objectivity
Like a great ritual vessel
Lost but floating free

Stock water disguise functions
You pay for the freedom
To come with me
Water and brain chemistry

Wine brandy apples rosin
Cork paper toys perfumes
Oil pitch tar oak pewter
Linen silk lace salt gin

Good loam soil weighs
Eighty pounds a cubic foot
Clay carries a strong negative electric
Charge so things cling to it

Poem

Face to face and in the face
These are the misleading susceptibilities
Tensed and caressing in a mixture
Nothing human but shaped by light

Caught then a word whistling up to spend
Or to spend some time together
A somber brush or melancholy blossoming
Through the curious to the vehement attitude

A lethal parallel right through say
The hypnotist's lie and the long and short of the song
Contriving chance or suppressing an abrupt notion
Expressionless retorted the reflective bread

Garb and garbled charms contrast shrill strokes
Top down and across to the right or up from the left
To the top no higher but to the upper right
No plateau no reach just the parallel reflected

Forbearing the given and its little distance
Then a vapor anticipating the spectacle
The suspect modulated obtaining silence with a gesture
Fresh points of platitude rising in columns of black smoke

Stranger than questionable or what is amplitude
In more than probable crouched in a corner
Some restless scrutiny confounds the offensive modesty
Liking the rule that corrects the emotion

The Table

Not wide but a wing
Balancing a sphere
Dissolving in a reward
Of fog— conversation's
Beard of light

Interest reaches
And there are large white plates
Indicators
Wintering
Tall glasses and a bowl of salt

Cold but agreeable
The place for it
The abstract agriculture of stones
The extended hand and
Bent neck of the earnest pilgrim

Just a hand around the curve
Once enough
And to believe
An accident
In the dark

The Anecdote That Went with It

The long reaches of the street.
Everything in order.
Pull it.

First the food.
Then the politics.
Not so much anymore.

Maybe. Maybe
Not. Maybe not.
Fails to flatter the prospects.

Folds against the seams.
It tightens off.
Blood flows.

The opposite shore the
Consequence of its own
Notion of righteous scrutiny.

It's what's done. It's
Just what's done.
That's all that's it.

But a reasonable solitude
Is a matter of months
Not a new man proposal.

The old symphony story
Looking right into the light
Is ink. Specters.

The edges of the shapes of color.
A chrome weasel a loam curve.
Vapors and self-fix hoodoo.

There they are moving slowly.
Stalks gathering. Stalkers.
Sunlight.

He was talking about the essential
Language only reminding us of pain
Tale told tale heard tale told heard.

Ripe Tack

Keel's echo small stagger
Float ridges load
Of old oaken stupors

Cool gravity local worth
Small room a cell a cabin
balanced in guilds

Scrawl of fields
acre and banner
flower and arrow

Hadrian's Lane

What fills the whisper and
all want fragments why along to check
the short page what your convictions
this is shudder and this is antenna mail

Not from here like a lot of wax lost wax
in fact misplaced the emptying the song
finishers indexing the aces ring phone
and circulate here and there a wave or

Something much harder for sleep like dance
rendering the up trace or cross cowers
for a bow makes for silence the big
polar wag the shift heads to roam

The volume cores the abject delirium of
capital the compressors fill from middle out
with a weird blue light too much focus on
the night too few stars a big chunk of it

How inert the dutiful to stare right into
how inflected as it were to bend or shape
from a straight to a narrow this is the way
from however to how best you hound the path

Remote air logic to take the measure
from ether logic to casual fulcrum block
can it go up and out into that remoteness
strain to the then and then and then softer flight

Well it seems there's a drubbed restraint
makes for the go road and empty bit of hum
nice target maybe or perspective's arena
squared in the calm wake of looksee

And then has a gander for totals
sprints the high street and makes for the fog
number shadow clue and mark it from rut to rut
frost heaves apprehend then the gallery of trees

Appetites tug at the argument and mood freight
a brain nab for smooth talk addlers of give go
all so much carbon the think's gummed
coordinated like currents but breaks the ankle

Obdurate wince to scuff the instanter
the junk prick cracking the ellipse
so now it's how you say an oval and hung
in a corrosive pose you get at it prying

JAMES SHERRY

Drawing on Kreisler

       He strings the separate nor near you
reach out reach to blind
when blind to the rest
       And were you five, Gitana, your palm
on Saint Sophia's rough stone when the old woman
hissed you back   the skin on your nape
contracts in shadow   soften your gaze toward
       The narrative then would regal us
Twist by the fire   gallop over the bark
you flutter and escape   the fricative flutter
       Say g for t and come and we will
Tanto through 1921 and into
your boudoir where the deep
red glass to the meniscus
       Can you can you
alphabet a breath
you surge in young aspire   to your lips bend
in the arbor   I who can barely speak to you
that so whisk by   Harmonic, harmony
sweet sweet come to our childhood
       Out of the child eye o naughty note

Drawing

for Bob Routch

I.

Fingers tremble over the belly
in whose round lurk the tangled brass
dragons curling up your leg
as you sit between two corpulent
men in overcoats, tickling the curve
of your calf and the circular
cloaca and the spit key.

II.

Call with zephyrs; puff your cheeks o'er curling crests.
Make men war, maids to marry, hounds to hunt
all through alloy, conch and horn; make ships heel to blue.
Though bitter clouds and fatigue appall, you
will not flag; your gleaming pennant cracks.

III.

What is it breathes
            out the mouth,
                through elbows and floodlights stars,
mounting by keys
            the tortuous route
        to the gentling hand,
        to the bell and ear?

What is it breathes
      where cat laps a pool of black
      and where it gets vent
filtering upward
      in a flood of fruit
   through bone and allegro,
   even unto rest?

The Word I Like White Paint Considered

   Anonymous days transact to know
   the poppies on the mauve river
   by narrowing down their trenches
   like soldiers inhale tenuous
   at a fruit stand fingering oranges and figure,
   ubiquitous from South Korea to Zaire,
   they're not in thrall or starving on the farm
   and therefore haven't been truncheoned themselves,
   before I come to where a special knock
   lets me in your movie house,
   who blackout trying on gloves
   with soft words inhering in ransom notes
   cut from advertisements that arrive in brown
   paper covers whose bedrooms are too hot,
   whose halls smell and strain awareness.

Hound's Nest for a Parafen

When the wind patch
who winter follows
    shhh
and tell of.
as if it

    tine
    plastic
        whaa
wheat storm
            who'll
    belly wop
          white birch angles
but no which way
*
All out
    snow on snow
        shsh
    phone call crumbles
aloof out
    deep snow
        sss
    oats thrive
        with ululation

About

This is about about, until now a subject reference, point of interest or city all roads converged upon. This is about about; to say what it's about and to be about it on all sides, around its house, in circuit, around the outside, here and there, approximately, almost, also includes a reversed position, in rotation, colloquially, near, in the vicinity, all round, in the neighborhood, not far from, on the verge of as a gerund (about being), concerning, but no longer "the subject" or what it's "about," more in the original sense of outside. It is the indexed subject, a space of nouns, persons in action, the words that pertain to their vicinity and intention or set them off by opposition. Space is made for a subject by delineating around it. The subject is what's left over: Not the thing, but what's about it.

Such non-referential and abstract modes express characteristics: for example, beauty is about ends, the spaces between our points of view, that is, about the corruption that fosters it—a possibility not out of line with traditional notions of transience. This is presented as an alternative to narrative creation, clothes that do not fit or are artified to appear to fit. The emperor's new clothes concealed nothing, and one can see now he is naked.

Nothing

That of which many large varieties are found in the major cultural centers of the United States. Although the eminent Earl of Rochester, John Wilmot, has somehow ascertained that Nothing was the elder sibling of Shade and spoke to it as to a familiar, the more modern variety seems unrelated to anything in particular, itself derived from nothing and going in that direction from which it came.

Nothing, as implied above, is derived from nothing, although translators of Hindu and Buddhist literature have more often found nothing to be a prefix of Ness, unrelated to the Scottish monster, which is only nothing coincidently. In colloquial terms nothing is what one has "plenty of," and it would not behoove any compilation of contemporary learning and culture to omit.

Nothing has been called dust, void, eternity, but in reality shirks all these aliases in modern times as being metaphysical, preferring the contemporary tendency to ascribe importance to the particular and objective; hence the modern tendency to make it a noun or person, making light of it by "little" or much of it by "big," the latter of which in this increasingly hectic age has tended to thrive more than the former.

Symbiosis

This poem's about somebody else, not me—
my brother, for instance, or my other
brother. Anyone imagination
can inhabit (Yeats' wife mouthing his dreams,
elephants leading a circus;
lichen; Tetons together: anyplace
but where I am) can stretch to fill the vacancy
that many images of sleep impressed.
With little bother I can stick my nose
in an affair and smother at my ease.
Another's death makes me proud to be alive.
I forget that I too am mortal,
being in the crush of my gratefulness.

No Chance Operations

He had a stroke of luck
where beasts lick their paws
of your armchairs and the fortune
cookie right eye of your surprising
spectacles carries the word
like Typhoid Mary, dragging bones
through green felt enough
that rien ne va plus.
His last words, "Utah Shale and Advanced Ross,"
smile where bubbles burst.

RAE ARMANTROUT

Extremities

Going to the Desert
is the old term

"landscape of zeros"

the glitter of edges
again catches the eye

to approach these swords!

lines across which
beings vanish / flare

the charmed verges of presence

Double

So these are the hills of home. Hazy tiers
nearly subliminal. To see them is to see
double, hear bad puns delivered with a wink.
An untoward familiarity.

Rising from my sleep, the road is more
and less the road. Around that bend are pale
houses, pairs of junipers. Then to *look*
reveals no more.

Latter Day

1

When the particular
becomes romantic—

blue bird,
green nut,
thin beak!

2

Porthole
in stucco,
bungalow—

like forgetting
what I meant.

3

In your absence, dear sir, this acquired
a wild salience.

4

A stillness as if
someone's finished speaking—

evening shadows
under carpet swirls.

Through Walls

Stomach: lonely.

Curled up in the
familiar ring
she went to sleep.

What a world, little churl!

Raw grass blades and
these spear-headed weeds,
dishevelled.

           Sun glancing.

Heat
did not
come home

to whom?

As if porous . . .
            Passing through

       * * *

Hungry for a garden's
whispered care.

Those blues and pinks.

           Who has
saved some for you

may part
the afternoon from an evening
looked to, and
looking back
or down on our
walled-off suspense.

"There's more," we are
to understand.

Excreting one more
link, and putting
a leaf back
on either side, a fin, a stroke, this
slow progress.

* * *

The awful thing
if every spurt
left him—

Anonymous Phrase—

in here   and there it
surfaces
under the hidden eyes of
Brer Fox and Brer Bear.

"Nana, na, nana."

* * *

Ready tongue.

Coming back at
her sister, then
willing
to address the world's
intelligent and
uninhabited designs.

Most at home when
well-known
words come through
the metal
wires, the unseen
"transformers"

saying
". . . reminds me of my home
far away."

Necromance

Poppy under a young
pepper tree, she thinks.
The Siren always sings
like this. Morbid
glamor of the singular.
Emphasizing correct names
as if making amends.

Ideal
republic of the separate
dust motes
afloat in abeyance.
Here the sullen

come to see their grudge
as pose, modelling.

The flame trees tip themselves
with flame.
But in that land
men prized
virginity. She washed
dishes in a black liquid
with islands of froth—
and sang.

Couples lounge
in slim, fenced yards
beside the roar
of a freeway. Huge pine
a quarter-mile off
floats. Hard to say where
this occurs.

Third dingy
bird-of-paradise
from right. Emphatic
precision
is revealed as
hostility. It is
just a bit further.

The mermaid's
privacy.

Range

There cloud moves in front of cloud, and above, suggesting
a deep breath, enormous range—such that a young girl
could leave home.

Long wind. Birds splutter and croak.
The difference now, she explains, is that she does not
lose consciousness when another takes the floor.

Who felt the vertigo of bouncing when he saw the fly
land on the leaf?

Who said, "Unnatural?"

The actress—the nun—the kid—the gatekeeper.

One harps continually
because she may have missed her cue.

"One notion, recognizable, with temperament and bluster
for real."

P. INMAN

Colloam

for Michael Sappol

morrow every listen
ago potato who have a paper voice
the hole where the effort went
tome is crayern
a fasten into trance, necklace some awake of notes, floorer
as classed some follow

looking glass parma
time to fulfill legs

proclair
spaim fasten, doubtbook
kettle about instincts, pylon as shininess
person cranberry
muriel of themes
holes in bruit, rubber another

happen not yet teeth
brule imogen

panelling up a breadline

fenimore morrow, recently lou reed
pickerel, cairo

hue frimmer in writing
every glue to her skin

mallowed the air around Tom Paine, farina almost a polaroid
brule italy acre
potato think of fenimore
either explain wet chaw
amass toward voice, in the same fieldstee
what at word

pilsen almond of know

pineal hear
imogen peebles, rubber cyclone was merely opinion
a mallow each flesh

now's the midnight i should have told
hang immode
ever texture a jelly, heightening out as clasp
talk in dense (marrow her tears)
the by hers, moat needed a guthrie
a raise in pour
persons at one loud
models my brain in paper money

could the calmed in louds
cup for cup a keeps
jaw lower than its walk to the jukebox
extra body to tier

kuwait insides
(reads are somewhat lessened)

from *red shift*

silos all by a stillness / nells from bend, a boil allow /

clock odd rounded by person / the pour in a wave off of sugar /

"roundheads overpass" / surd balls. / all that muscle in

blackboard, ocean propos / did i read it on a page or look

ahead about print exactly alike / divides (every) to a blue

now or less of a forest / all the time in a pause, pointed

inland / lewt marsh add / a date based on still air /

name can't stick all that treeline / lemp synod / how after

is all / ever since "white blood", a rise etched at her /

how far back would an idea go / palatine of paper

pickerel think / sunken sky to frizz / up collapse /

divides to a blue leaned ink / style is just each, the side

beneath dates / coda geller / the city-line of a personage

/ chest wall less as skelter / "mour" "baleen" "in-

digo" / indigo none each Cowper's gland / mute wooler

prose as one long stage direction / how exact a volume open

to a place / humped piano, shorelines equal by their over,

hayed down alors / earth Gogh than truth / stacked talk

to a soda (dipster) / standing legged the wrong amount to

pronounce. page shows of its better midst / sawtooth, dreth

BOB PERELMAN

Book Years

A religious virgin of unspecific sex
Opens the book again. Great trees
Mass into a risen gloom. Green
Valleys bathed in blue light lull
A scattered population. The world ends;

A person is born, no sense
Thinking about it forever. I'm writing
While time stands still. It certainly
Doesn't lead to the future. First
In a series of willing abstractions,

The body makes history and leaves
No one to clean up after
It's gone. Flesh mirrors its absence
In solid colors; generations absorb finite
Amounts of light. Identity is abbreviation.

A religious frenzied realism leaves no
Place to go, no stone unturned.
An aesthetic pharmacopia of diseases projects
Fuzzy slides of a beautiful woman
Living forever in perfect health, dancing

On rocks, acres, dark green world.
She's only a figure of speech,
But the books, the modern library
Giants, fall beneath her feet. Lives
Accumulate sound like clouds hold water.

Primer

for Alan Bernheimer

The surface of the earth displays
A grain of sand. The pace it keeps
Creates bonds of love that stretch
Past the breaking point. Matter
Resents nothing. Plants try.
Animals can barely think. Speaking

Their minds, people load the air
With noise so thoroughly meant
That a would-be heaven
Falls from the sky and is
Where we follow our wills
To lead our lives, chasing

Bent actions along the curve
Of a finite door. The equations
Produce curbed or unleashed powers,
Barking into a dark garage

Or surviving the face of the deep.
For the earth to revolve
Continuously requires constant
Vigilance, endless sleep.

Seduced by Analogy

First sentence: Her cheap perfume
Caused cancer in the White House late last night.
With afford, agree, and arrange, use the infinitive.
I can't agree to die. With practice,
Imagine, and resist, use the gerund. I practice to live
Is wrong. Specify. "We've got to nuke em, Henry"
Second sentence: Inside the box is plutonium.
The concept degrades, explodes,
Goes all the way, in legal parlance.

"I can't stop. Stop. I can't stop myself."
First sentence: She is a woman who has read
Powers of Desire. Second sentence:
She is a man that has a job, no job, a car, no car,
To drive, driving. Tender is the money
That makes the bus to go over the bridge.
Go over the bridge. Makes the bus. Tender
Are the postures singular verbally undressed men and women
Assume. Strong are the rivets of the bridge. "I'm not interested,
Try someone else" First sentence:
Wipe them off the face. Not complete.

Bold are the initiatives that break deadlocks
In the political arena of sexual nation states.
A bright flash I, the construct, embrace all my life
All the furniture in Furniture World, U.S.A.,
All my life on tv "first thing in the morning."
My head is, somewhere, in my head. Say, threaten,
Volunteer, want, all take the infinitive.
First sentence: The woman's clothes volunteered
To mean the woman's body. Biology
Is hardly the word. No irony, no misleading
Emphasis, just a smooth, hard, glossy desktop.

The President was "on the ceiling."
He could watch himself face down the faceless forces of history.

A nation's god is only as good as its erect arsenal.
It's so without voice, in front of the face, all my life I,
In corners, dust, accumulating rage breaking
Objects of discourse. "Why use words?" Smells from
The surrounding matter, the whole tamale.
"I have no idea" "I use my whole body"
"Be vulnerable" First sentence: They were watching
The planes to fly over their insurgent hills.
Second sentence: Their standard of living
We say to rise. No third sentence.

Word World

Gentle analogists rock the surface
of the inhabitable word. *I*
am the earth, the sun, the moon
the taste of bread, the place

of sex and death. That's why
there are tears at weddings, jokes
at funerals, and animated projections at birth.
Doesn't logic depend on tact?

And if reality has toes to be stepped on
I have whole Patagonias of emotional red ink
taught to the rule of a spiritualized
virtu-laden hickory stick, strict, unspeakable
bodies dying to pronounce its name.

Streets

There's no history in the past.
Nothing happens there anymore.
A brown twilit civic peace
oozes mesolithically from the clumps of ancient houses.
The narrow alleyways are collagenous
a mat of dusty humus nourishing
the squat human stalks. Fake sky gods
take care of the plot.
By the end, Pinocchio is a real boy.

At its première, history was received poorly.
Catharsis was a slap in the face
as the spectators watched themselves
being measured, killed, inflamed, conscripted, armed to the
        teeth, inventoried, invented, in a word
loaded onto the train.

the face, race, fate—words blurred
in the upset crowd noise—
something, at any rate, was suddenly precious
torn, out of reach, available
at a price, too high to pay.

For the general populace, it was discrete
leftover images: newspapers stacked on the back porch, the smell
        of the Chinese restaurant spreading across the
        tracks and the reddish-green sumac
episodic, meaning less & less after each commercial.

It is on these unmaintained tracks
that the stories, Ann Landers, *Dynasty*, the shapes of the cars
arrive in the form of a thoughtless city
run by minds whose characters (the letters of the name)

are complete, not to be altered
certainly not by what happens.

The towers are visible from far away.
The land beneath is valued at the inhabitants' food shelter &
    transmission of

lacunae the soft shredded pages go here
between the rows of traffic.

Binary

Two heads are better than one.
Sunlight on the grass is better
than the power to dissolve oneself
into a variety of blades.
The declarative sentence
cut
lash die kill interrogate clear away
the blood-soaked body
no longer here the declarative sentence
would be something other than what it
says except that "you are what I am"
is to "the unspoken forces that surround us"
as "sunlight," see above, is to
"mental furniture," trashed, sat on
in state, loved, its wheels licked far into the night
sirens, thighs, the whole gizmo going off
or not
and then why bother, except
already bothered on both sides

Finally the I writing
and the you reading (breath still misting the glass)
examples of the body partitioned by the word.
Pie in the sky, tons, suspended
over one's heads
by a single declaration of desire.

A tragic curse
is dripping down generations
making mincemeat of the fully grown and operational
person, whose mother
may have said goodnight in the violet light
projected down the individual hall
in such a way that novel
was complete
inside that gesture.
All it needed were other people
in sufficient quantity
and limited lifespans.

In realtime drama, however, people suck
and what eventually lets down
is some earlier story
they only find out about later
chopped to bits somewhere barely on the map.
The spectators, duly echoing
in the amphitheater, must find
what identities they can.

BRUCE ANDREWS

And the Love of Laughter

What he lent itself   Studious   Of blind faith

Is a commemorative   And exclamations   Coups of hashish

     Anti-clericalism detect   & the mirror image

An ideal so seriously   dah-dah-dee   And the tone when

door   Who promptly dries up   Her sex congratulatory

     And envy too   Spurt   Repeats every   Turned

mistrustfully to fools   Makes that imperative   A

wryness

     Has skin instead

     Against Ngo Dinh Diem

     With its millenarian overtones

     A rich skimming of cream

     What would defies quick

     Disparity between *what* and *how*

     A special courage syrup

     Given unusual beauty

     Of violating kindergarten canons

     In number hits or learning curve slopes

     Seeking slender

     Lifts its Gothic lace

To have platonically in love

Aimed at producing mixture

The buoyant particularities

Grace torn between simply disparate ideals

Overlap even where least needed

Romantic will accuse me

A negative   were it not too serious   answered by a put

man   must be quite perverse   the gymnasts of naughty

influencing health   social health   wants to unite *with*

as expressions of class   interested   spins lies out

of his own entrails   but we misread such gnomic passages

am sure of the sureness   elaborate costume

and always behaved like one   sought sin out   and once

breezy in memory   was premature   include servants

a penumbra of impressions   and relinquishes the habit so

suffers a confusion of sexual identity   fancies linger on

being wet weather norm blue orchids   worried less about

the right word and his cloak-and-dagger band   there's no

best better way   always go   man by nature good

regretted behaving   to reduce to rational frame much of

irrationality involved   squirreled a mixture   moving

vertically   is the exclusionary exclusion   the baby-

talking ingenue   given unusual collaborative power

all express   oil   and youth an asset too   that

complete breakdown of personal pride   rich skirting of doubt

ink of excellent quality   to roast another battery

with his equally impassioned letters   the gradually
diminishing size of the borders   crazy quilt   held
incommunicado   putrid   and streak of lightning
I doubt we shall again   so typical to be happy   and
communal solidarity   leaped from the cock to the asse
  a brought-to-life sawhorse   persistent womanizer
steps are reminiscent   to the level of revelation   of
life   are histrionic   in prison slang   courtesy
most unbuttoned historic   does not mean contempt   and
syntax   Islam   is a quality motive   and wicker
impartiality   puppy circumstance   where they fly up
   are sociological horses of wood   and the casual handling
      culture have their hen head here indeed   sweetness if
composed   says a word is no strategy   was gig-lamp eyes
      to justify all means   a context & vibrato
through instrumentalized material progress   light   of
lame pastiche   ethnomethodology   these mock heroics
      the pleasure   ask the right embarrassments   of
inflicting a syphilitic   culture-bound by the dozen
episode by episode   the real grief has been displaced
   of personal insurance   into the arms   rare   as
an *in*halation   the skids   dismissed as 'old shit'
   into the arms of language   a vast multiplication
thank you don't choice   a vast multiplication   who
promptly reverts to longitude   to inculcate the real is it
dispersed presence as often   somnambulant   to ad lib

as attested   platonic grenadiers   the Antichrist

    in the Auto da Fés   such alibis   at the slit

hecatombs   the withheld breath   us down inside upside

down   to treat you bad   a comic sidelight   almost

singlehandedly   when asks point-blank with fever

putative   the word 'robot'   defend but deeply felt or

agitated but saturate   pierce the windbags   in mummy

communist oil drums   fulfills a determinate function

to glorify the vernacular   silt   stalls a dim boy

    a sneering sing-song   unreminded   to get personal

assurance of American support   is larded with or hop with

self-congratulatory   the   prophetic enigma   haloed

mytheme   to harmonize them   animate paper dolls

    of patent medicine   is a response of expulsion

with telescopic sight perilously close on   makes them least

improper   who takes them off the page   as expressions

of material intent which are curious and circularly unfolded

    bastard says imprimatur   concealing is no stratum

    in a desultory way   nor its replacements in tin

worrying could not — foretold   and that is that that every

story   a gross distortion of speech   a single humbling

    bubble   to think everything   softened

to revive in its own terms   perhaps irreparably damaged

    whose behavior had analogies   by generosity

active compass   what they were not   and the love of

laughter

Matter of Fact

Sanity be applicable something men

But entails bridge energy often left me know to do with

Fabric may predict what experience

Custom rears itself 2 sides foresee both change intimate nothing
in the files

Hesitance colors — uppermost green middle yellow — get coffee to
make sense paper out of Abyssinia residue left illusion choice
such a reading compensating to interdict what she driving at what
I meant I want

Now

Lay horizontal to analogy back down how *you* reciprocate so am
confused makes pursuit gelatinous purpose

Have to work your body lattice of semantics whisk off

Lines eviscerate by sensitivity to terminology takes me home

And end an arm inhabits of desire plethora on hood by twos found
textured itself back here again peripeteia shadow back in limb
crook to permit causes court bi-valved in previous sympathy kisses
recur locatable dovetails beguine for real you hold

We mention profligate

Back in time

Face valley of validity

Route package

Am tangential

Yet *anytime*

While

were I idiom and

the portray

what on

idiot you remarking

cessed to only up

opt hope this

was soundly action

more engineer

taut that the

that in of the oolong

into offers

bedless

this of accent guiles

causation

the against as

liberators

for it outside

the until nascent

the within on

an intent

and of depicts

from *Confidence Trick*

Equality demands no less; history begins with old man crying, logic you know, airplay your fingertips is not freedom — The disintegrating slop situation on outlaw; read it in the voodoo prospectus, keep trying death squads paid for by our *Christianity* radiation taxes so that human rights clone improves because there are so few rebels left to kill, like iron filings — Polkadot mentality you capsulize it with a commemorative stamp, slunk down in the heroic mode for comfort, Belfast, Capetown, compose loonee tunes that could be written in the mind by institutional simpletons

Aesthetics pension comes first; dry business to do battle with easy embalming business, mistake rut-pink, impatient nauseating nerve — Plastic Babylon is the joint, digital dance, you have got garbage, bad fountain of youth flanked by giant horses: pygmy redemption — Wavelength is only curious to die; preemptive redemption — Brain rockabilly, anarchy out demographics itself

I m sorry, we had a technical problem with the words, punks are the old farts of today — Peacock throne is crumbling, I prefer the aerial attacks, leather complex; have a bonus self-esteem fix, here is the ocular proof — Mormons are fighting about secession, cipher drones, sedate sex appeal of the inorganic; bomb shelter branch plant, quintessentially as if subtitled by blowhards — He wants to *force out* its meaning; brief crud — With mass allegiance?: what s that weird humming in the background?: yeah, but into flowering odorama? — The tongue is ink, the genitals are paper, pit one Indian detox center against another I.R.A. one, just like your mom, I prefer the aura — Letters cremate each other in reverse — Undulating uniform, oratory methodology all the monkeys; in Latin America, abortion is legal only in Cuba — Ulcer is not bootlaced up — Spill blood on the nosecones — They examine specimens of fine breeding, dictatorship on local option, in what realm are we supposed to be activists? — Fuchsia rayon; you talk too much; I resent danger; what room do iron laws have for social change? — Well, all of them are talented so it s only a question of who sells out the most successfully

Those naughty lumps — The young will not be *vitaminized* any longer, the future is theirs, how decorous is the sugar beet? — Ignore bass spitefully, depilatory secret is in a fix, bag of intestines, handy dandy heaven up here — What *were* the great books? — I went want went out does nothing to rehearse I want went want out, so, so what did you think *were, normal?* — I hate memorizing things; crispy ambulance, mom didn t feel comfortable enough to astonish us; it is a blimp with a gland problem — Floodlights too old to

Eat his ashes; miraculously at an exact rose — The genetics industry will relieve all of our Malthusian anxieties

I m turning myself into a sofabed warehouse — Loop, new hormones; strafing, don t try to cure yourself — Teachers pet = fools gold = rents due — I m not arbitrarily fronting this, I m not talking about Punch & Judy; we ve decided to call you to the psychiatric panel — *Am I not Christian?* — A model airplane should look like a real airplane — You should do that in gay bars, in S & M bars more generally — Praxis with a combo is restricted code, O.K., so repeat same history on my body, is tease degree blood 'taking action'; we wear workboots to predate our anxiety — In order to become a book, who *is* or who *is* literate; we don t perform *Heroin* anymore; peeping tom sex for tonight

Translate that — Dyslexia — The white suburban kids couldn t handle it, detective work, listened to mariachi music, who wore zoot suits — sedated the shills; Heathcliff, you re *never* out of danger, people thinking into the radio, latent benefits for famous junkies — I found the lost coordination — Poke it up, error like that; hook & legal drone — Rifles = statemental merrygoround — Balloon rules misspelled in a book — Marijuana tastes like *boiled* clams — I don t like people that much, do you?

BARRETT WATTEN

"X"

Start anywhere.

Alarms. Concentric rings.

All mirrors in corners. Fragments cluster. Heaps.

The writer after his words are dead.

". . . after the bomb's dropped."

Stick figures against ground.

Time passes.

"Their fate is to remain."

Output, delete. Scratch on copper plate.

An alphabet pointed towards . . . A utopian index
condensed to . . .

Syntax erased.

Mist floats over glass.

An artifact is a mistake.

"Ibis guards over young flesh." Terror of . . . Texture of . . .

Explain.

"Density, condensation is the key . . ." The key to the city, a slap in the face.

No excuses.

The first in a series of . . . Attention, depth of betrayal.

I was born where . . .

Roads approach. Fountains at the base.

"Impenetrable but direct."

Stops.

A man reads his magazine while . . .

Units. Notes to . . . Everything else is suppressed.

Springs. Echoes of . . .

Standard design.

A state of well-being where . . . It's dangerous to leave.

Seen through the eyes of . . .

Items, each.

Bas-reliefs, burnt-out residua of . . . Their vernacular base.

Windows on . . . Wide asphalt. A boxed set of . . . Parquet floors.

The car starts. Alternating down the street.

". . . could put them together but . . ."

Second generation. Out-of-focus lens.

Increments of . . . Imagined light, accumulates. Plains of . . .

The time it takes to get there. Delays.

Traffics cross.

The middle ground under one flag.

"Toy Division—American Motors." Then they are told . . .

The weather's better, out of this world.

Repeats.

Clarity, outline of . . .

Buildings, a field, background, the sea.

Melting. Rooted to the spot.

Low white clouds, stucco yellow blocks.

"But you are the dream."

Observation tower over excavation site.

As far as . . . Occluded by . . . Facing backwards across . . . While looking to the side . . .

Instinct. Technique.

And drives straight ahead.

Homes.

There are no pictures here. I speak as if . . .

Formica table, rheostat lamp, speckled ceiling, cut glass.

Bric-a-brac. The cube.

Everything meant is to be seen.

An animated facade . . . The spectators within.

Replicates.

Topology of . . . A stepwise advance, progression against . . . A permanent grid.

That broad, vague roads traverse.

Drained swamps and emptied rivers.

Into the heart of the original city.

"There it is, take it." Anything can be said of it is true.

There's no alternative but . . . Complete surrender of . . .

Misplaced records. Routes marked in advance.

Close-ups of . . .

Memory keys. Multiples, mistakes. One and any number.

A fact is what you can't get past.

Long public buildings, vertical light through clouds.

Axis of . . . Division, dissolves.

A simple reflex, change of address.

Mode Z

Could we have those trees cleared out of the way?
And the houses, volcanoes, empires? The natural
panorama is false, the shadows it casts are so many
useless platitudes. Everything is suspect. Even
clouds of the same sky are the same. Close the door
is voluntary death. There is one color, not any.

Prove to me now that you have finally undermined
your heroes. In fits of distraction the walls cover
themselves with portraits. Types are not men. Admit
that your studies are over. Limit yourself to your
memoirs. Identity is only natural. Now become
the person in your life. Start writing autobiography.

Mimesis

It thinks, permanent address, states, stands apart, exits
    Blocked, nets governing alphabet that to one point
Strain in procedure yields an increment in prose, a skeleton
    Giving birth emits artificial sparks, finding terminal
At one end, an irregular mosaic stretching out to hinge
    Breaking pattern through caesura, distances stopped
Soundings isolate, cut off in air on condition that brick
    Picture suits only this building, entrances following
To mark a figure no longer needed to speak English . . .

The analogy lies in each language, contrary to surface
    Revealed: "The coefficient is nothing but a souvenir
Pulse needle tone, a stop, half-made difference between
    Something about, simply one unit of length solidified
In conventional rods, displacing as it pleases, straightening
    The form either of unit stress, name of metal or fog of
Reactive light, pump suction, returning force equally delayed
    Transforming apparent weight, depressing its center
While waiting, cued, it falls asleep as it goes up . . ."

Assemble blocks, ramps, heaps, nets, prop them up with broken
    Equipment, an elastic language one could translate
Into good photos of a table standing upright on level ground
    Color, shape, height, size are revised and corrected
"Is it speakable?" while underneath the utensils a dictionary
    Where each word connects by friction free from baby talk
Through sieves to argue knots from dizziness, word crossed out
    Becomes what of theory with stills of very large objects
Close up their extrinsic molds cut by imagined planes . . .

Find scenery to be used in this film, magnify from distance
    A matrix of wandering eyes returning to perspective
Irregular reservoir retaliating from height of notes taken
    Bullet trajectory passing through a stack of cards . . .

The parabola given to represent this is dotted as they burst
    Into actual dimensions, a cube one could move around
Struck from the mass, made into a package, the enhancement
    Of background light silhouettes figures, stacks, floor
To ceiling correspondence of moving parts to fictitious base . . .

Virtue of partition speaks, a starting point set off by
    Weights and measures among primitive forms, light
Because the eye goes around the cloud, deforming its curve
    Fixing itself in a pole common to all, a penknife
In one's fist, bright orange flares, center of gravity
    Reversing nouns and verbs, walking into screen, wheels
Blossoming cylinders compress atmosphere held in place
    To power certain machines, constant change of density
Opens way for attack, bombs on fields, waterfalls, stencils . . .

"The other did not die, the other was involved in a game
    Myself was very divided from itself then, compulsively
Repeating plastic or logical necessity by filling in forms
    Which needed boundaries, a key cut out ahead of time
Needing an argument, an explosion better to shrink away from
    But looking at it in daylight was grey, uneven tones
Completely spread out, distortion casting shadows
        simultaneously
    All over, indicating movement across wide fields
Without knowing it, I myself created a loophole to escape . . ."

It is certain that every word it speaks travels in space
    Virtually attacked by echoes tangent to sound by analogy
One would like to get around, speaker seen in profile so that
    Timed retorts disappear into tone, emancipated bays
Filling in with standard illumined sets, upright at liberty
    Wishing for what stared directly at, quote mirror erratum
The glass eye loses the thread, grammar's symmetrical image
    Going around a radius revising the eye, the end of the line
A hinge, a jet of water undergoing little change of shape . . .

Once learned thought vanishes, producing checkmate by parts
    A luxury item plays surface to return exactness of input
Firing off authorizations in actual size to demultiply
    Continua cut into luminous prototype, inventing address
Or its apparition if exhausted, a stream of uniform elements
    Could be this coherent sentence, ascending spinal column
Searching out retinal charge, opaque black paper, solar fruit
    A priori contraries in serial jumps from one to ten
Could hide this little man, having no intention to be useful . . .

Relays

Let no one consider the original noise.

Outside there's noise. Time doesn't print.

A bar of sulfur lies on a mahogany table. From this point to the
frontier is exact.

This distance between yourself and what you are intended to see.

Steam-driven pilings hold up the bridge like logs under the feet
of sunburnt slaves rolling I-beams to their designated resting
place on a riverbank in Kansas.

Romantic ideas take over. The bridge is easily missed.

Then they drive it into the ground.

I can't believe that I'm actually alive at this time and place. Many
can do better than that.

In this elaborate projection which makes you fall asleep.

Thought emerges from its all-inclusive wrapper. A workman pounds the wall into shape with his fist.

In obscure wording he announces his fate to a questioner.

The sentence-producing mechanism cannot be permitted to operate unchecked.

A large young woman sobs in a steaming hot bath.

In the library in which I find myself, exteriors are the master plan.

Absence is used as a word. "It is not to be found in imaginary facts."

There is massive unemployment in Europe. Columns of people move from a great distance down a long road.

This is background music.

Close-up of cartoon figure, his fleshy skull and top hat.

Intervals should be spoken aloud at foreign occasions. All thought captures toys.

Now match up things to their parts.

"I" quote myself.

"Pleasure is an engine like this one." A bent nail collapses into the pen.

Brief narratives ride away in the sight of the stuck person. The back of the man is attached to the crowd.

Mediators solve the problem.

Kings do not touch doors. The entire landscape is covered with pins stuck perpendicular to the ground.

My time spreads out and latches on to anything. They wait in secret for a searchlight to be directed on them.

Then the floor surges up.

Describe this to a person on a plane.

This is to make us inhabitants. A boat plows into the water, immediately met by waves.

An elastic web stretches from palm to palm. Hooks can be located in the brain.

Large grey ribbons package the report.

Machines eat into walls to produce other machines.

To make the train go forward we must push the cushions with our feet.

Up and up go figures of speech—to the summit.

These little stumbling blocks are the arguments of my fate.

Coins come into contact with hands, pockets, purses, and machines.

A small dog appears in the text.

I wish for something greyer. The small dog "translates" the rug.

I'd rather listen to madness.

In caves, the animal is a principle to protect the head.

Hats, chairs, ballooning dresses.

Disappointments raised whose opera-glasses?

Something in language doesn't want to budge.

This sentence is art and science. Not more than 10% conscious, the body itself has parts.

"While in use it is getting used up."

The letter T stands out. The most autonomous works of art are windows on the larger working mass.

Now he begins to read.

I approach some heavy black strokes printed on a placard. Impatience bursts out of fundamental blocks.

Separation burns from word to word.

"The lighting is uniformly blue. A brass wall surrounds the infant, an overturned bottle of ink."

Rolling with unwieldy vagueness, the motive is an endless wave.

"Gardens full of vicious hybrids and paradoxical grafts."

The terrible sky is bluer than usual. It will have to be done over again.

Something else corrects the narrative "answer." The agent of the dream is a slave.

The human interest is almost an aside.

But you can never get the glass out of the bottle.

The null sound is dead.

To my right an enormous, out-of-proportion Pekinese with red, fluffy fur has just disappeared around the corner of a building. Everyone laughs.

Translation: neither is there any kite which is fully aware of its string.

Any person in Egypt is not more permanent than this.

CHARLES BERNSTEIN

Senses of Responsibility

Of all these, pieces from which this
spoon, solitary as it is atop this table, a pen,
whatever other hang of discomfort, issues like
"please" & "thank you" & I forgot to mention
someone who will make you take offense at this
attic altogether, might as well as, forgive
some one or other stutters—what I most want
already has reformed itself & can't properly
stand up to what "I feel like" I will be able
to do. Actually, the rung, shades, consumable
beverages, typewriter keys, thermometer &
door stops all have been located but the
several other things—the names don't matter—
now begin to feel more pressing. Admonitions
about several trips to Turkey, about the Persian
rug in the other room, about "that light" glowing
outside the window "all night" only by the time
you stumble on it, panicking at the last minute
that it must be put out, large row houses have
replaced it, in which you must live. Whether by

train, car, bus or foot it takes longer than
expected but the delay has an aroma much to itself
that you can count on. Destinations don't, are so
quickly receding points. A visual imagination:
that what it takes discerns skyline from cluster,
handle from brim. I look over the side & find
it much the same. "Old hat," "shoe lace," "shag
carpet." Only you need to do so much more than
ever could be "expected" of you.

It's not that miracles are achieved, nor that we
make them happen as we sweep away all the
remnants of that other life we keep thinking is
the best one to possess. Starting from this
new spot, lakes acting as shifters for our understanding,
for that newer insight that always seems to be just
the same old one that keeps being forgotten. Switches
of tense are the tones that don't let us alone,
peeking out of the curtain, "hi" "thanks very
much I forgot to ask for that yesterday" "let's
get out of here." Much happens that never
gets properly decided upon & later it's obvious
that it had to be that way. Everything gets thrown off
balance, or, really, a constantly new balance is
achieved, only you wish the new equilibrium wouldn't

take over so fast. It's been too good a time but
always at the expense of the children.

Assuredly: not this same prattling, flutter, off in some
shell glamour, but marvelously largesse of demeanor &
coming over, without that hesitation inside that so plagues,
haunts, gives *"gnaw to"*—"this is the way it is & you've
simply to accustom yourself to it's own internal integrity."
Wind, chill, umbrellas, radio antennae—all had become vestigial
to our top priorities. A rain pouring down *next to* the house
but all this time we were with the neighbors, who could never
otherwise be reached. Elastic bands better off
in their own containers: a spring that by foreign measure
empties cups, frying pans actually, now made of glassine
substance: a large grey box in which slate floors no longer
feel at home. They talk it over, not even a
prayer of a chance is given for "that other principle" far
exceeding what any of us would care to demand. It's
not that . . . but *just that.* . . . &, pulling myself up
by my own linament, a smallish round tray that even now
gets misplaced, the same old pattern reveals itself. "The
pillow cases are all from Lord & Taylor but the sheets—
this will really blow you away—are from Simpson's, in
Toronto." Plastic discs that really don't care a whit
what *we* do, make of ourselves. Yet the lowest trees

have tops, skyrockets, & you pop into the very next

showing & say you're sorry to have been detained, while

harboring a colony of chickpeas in

place of your front lapel. "What a card he

is" refuses to submit to the usual procedure of

buckling down at the red flashing light, which not only

is not cause for celebration but practically necessitates

that the whole shop shut down. All eyes glaze

at the announcements, which sound more like an enjoinder—

not to worry. But this still to be encompassed in the

almost repressed instinct to let self-consciousness

pose in the guise of criticism. "I

got a neckache," "the joint's all akimbo"

but there's still one man left in this department

who can tell a syntagma from a peristalsis.

The noise swelled over the middle table

& a chiseled voice rose above it almost filling the room.

Sentences My Father Used

Casts across otherwise unavailable fields.
Makes plain. Ruffled. Is trying to
alleviate his false: invalidate. Yet all is
"to live out," by shut belief, the
various, simply succeeds which. Roofs that
retain irksomeness. Points at
slopes. Buzz over misuse of reflection
(tendon). Gets sweeps, entails complete
sympathy, mists. I realize slowly,
which blurting reminds, or how you, intricate
in its. This body, like a vapor, to
circumnavigate. Surprising details that
hide more than announce, shells codifiers to
anyway granules, leopards, folding chairs.
Tables at party which is no less the surprise
anyway in here fashion prizes. Straps,
everyday kind of stores. Ruminate around
in there—listens for mandatory disconsolation,
emit high pitched beeps. Not so inevitable as
roads which bear no signs. I guess eyeglasses,
motor cars piled up behind large—heap tall—pulleys,
regarding each other with mild affection, like
whose pushing these buttons, or a

walk in the park, by the lake, rivers discoursing

at length, which makes you much more

tired than thinking about it, the grass

taller than you imagined just before, rocks

nimbly rolling down sides of inclines. Or

how one day it became inevitable that

you would go back, hair blazing,

and start the walk down, careful to

look on both sides of the poplar lined street,

and with steady pace, don't even pretend to

recall, finally arrive. A large room in which

the people chat amiably—a hush that descends

even on leaves. "In a twinkle of an eye

it comes, the great secret which arrests

outer motion, which tranquilizes the spirit,

which equilibrates, which brings serenity

and poise, and illuminates the visage with

a steady, quiet flame that never dies." Shunning

these because of a more promising

hope of forgetfulness, I can

slip back in, see the wire coil making its steady

progress, peer at the looks flashed in my face. Best

leave that alone, & not make any noise either, lie by

the pool absorbed in its blue. "But we are not

equals; we are mostly inferior, vastly inferior, inferior

particularly to those who are contained, who

are simple in their ways, and unshakable in their

beliefs." Screens popping up every which way, embarking

us on our journey. Lessons learned, the pages

turned over. Crevices eaten away by misapplication,

subsistence, clamor. *It is our furniture that is*

lacking and our fortune that we are powerless.

Fortunate. The history of my suffering: useless

and. "Like we would have it today." Silk

hat. Which I never expressed at the time. My

sister Pauline, my brother Harry. Was very well

ah to me it was sad. That could have aggravated.

That may have brought on. The impression I got

is everybody. Or I should say well groomed. But

in appearances. Apoplexy. Any chance of accumulating

money for luxuries. Never even challenged,

never thought—that was the atmosphere we found

ourselves in, the atmosphere we wanted to

continue in. Exchange Buffet. Which is very

rare. Which I hear is not so apparent. Which

blows you away. Like the GE is here. We

don't fear this. It will quiet down. Now I

was not a fighter & I would run away but

they surrounded me & put

eggs in my hat & squashed them & I came

home crying & my mother said what are
you crying for if you go to the barber shop
you'd have an egg shampoo & here you
got it for nothing. Muted, cantankerous, as
the bus puffing past the next vacant question,
jarring you to close it down a little
more, handle the space with. "Now I'm going
to teach you how to sell goods." No rush or
push. We just conformed because of the
respect we had for each other. Sky scraped
by borders, telling you which way, I had
better advise, or otherwise looney
tunes appear in the hall &, glass in
hand, you debate the enclosures. A sultry
phenomenon—drained of all possibility to
put at ease, but heat soaked all the
same. Recursive to a fault. Lips eroded,
tableware carelessly placed as if the
haphazard could restore the imagination.
Instantly insincere. I told you
before: even current things: the
advancement of medicine, the new
chemicals that were coming up, the cures
that were starting to break through.
Patent leather shoes. In a gentle way. I

wasn't very, I didn't have a

very, my appearance wasn't one of, that

one could take, well I didn't make

the. Nothing stands out. Nice

type of people. Rather isolated. Pleasant.

I had the same dream constantly: swinging

from chandelier to chandelier. Crystal.

In a crowd of people. Just

local. In shame. Closeouts, remnants.

I don't remember too much. Gad

was on my back everyday.

I always figured: what I could lose.

Those were my values. To me they were

good values. I didn't want to

struggle. & I could live frugally. I didn't

want to get involved. I didn't care

for it. Necessity made the. Which

can't be helped. *Meeting us on our journey,*

taking us away. Hooks that slide past

without notice, only to find out too late

that all the time that transportation

was just outside the door. Sitting there.

I felt badly about it but never made a

protest for my rights. We never thought

of that. I kept in short pants: what

was given we ate. Nobody had
to tell me this. Everything went into
the business: being able to take advantage
of an opportunity, create an opportunity.
It was just a job I had to do.
We were separated all the time. No
rowdyism, no crazy hilarity. Impelled
sometimes beyond hands, that forces
otherwise in a manner of. Interesting
conclusions leaving you stripped of
subsistence, trimmed beyond recognition,
& all the time the tree lined roads—perfectly
spaced—mock the inner silence that voids all
things. To take a step—"I had to"—leading
without gap to a treasury of ambitions. "In
here" I am whole. Or goes over piles of
rocks—cowboy, pharaoh, bandit—stealing looks
across the street so often crossed but never
lingered in. With a sense of purpose divorced
from meaning. Strictly misrepresenting by it
this loom of enclosure, a path that opens onto
a field, lost on account of open space. Never
enough, randomly rewarded. I get way in, feel
the surface tight around the shape, breaks
through. A canvas of trumped up excuses, evading

the chain of connections. As so far bent
on expectation. "Don't stay in here, then."
Earned by driving mile over mile of eroded
insistence. The plane swoops down low over
the city, the gleaming lights
below waken the passengers to the possibilities
of the terrain, a comfortable distance above
& back into the clouds. A moisture that
retains hope, damp cellars of glass in which
large rectangular tubes carry passengers to
various levels, concavities really, endless
expanses of planes stacked on planes. Leaving
this place, so hugely exiled for whatever
bang of misprision you take the time out for,
a cacophany of shifts, tumbling
beside the manners you've already discarded,
falling among—in place of—them. The laugh
is worn out and you make your way amid
shocks and rebounds to the next counter,
allowing for the requisite number of "of course
you're right" "I never could have" "let's
try it again." Misled by the scent, you
spend the whole day trying to recover
what was in your pocket, the watch your
parent gave you if you would only mind

the hour. Months sink into the water and
the small rounded lump accumulates its
fair share of disuse. Dreadfully private,
pressed against the faces of circular
necessity, the pane gives way, transparent,
to a possibility of rectitude.

The Sheds of Our Webs

Floating on completely vested time, alacrity
To which abandon skirts another answer
Or part of but not returned.
Confined to snare, the sumpter portion
Rolls misty ply on foxglove, thought
Of once was plentitude of timorous
Lair, in fact will build around
It. Shores that glide me, a
Tender for unkeeping, when fit with
Sticks embellish empty throw. Days, after
All, which heave at having had.

Stove's Out

There is an emptiness that fills
Our lives as we meet
On the boulevards and oases
Of a convenient attachment. Boats
In undertone drift into
Incomplete misapprehension, get
All fired up inside. Altogether
A breeze down a long bounce
Furnishing behavior for buttons.
A wrinkle arrests an outline,
Streamers inquire the like of which
Nobody in reach has any idea
Of. Wonder to have been
Brought there, a plastic shift
Unseating a chiffon shock.

You

Time wounds all heals, spills through
with echoes neither idea nor lair
can jam. The door of your unfolding
starts like intervening vacuum, lush
refer to accidence or chance of
lachrymose fixation made
mercurial as the tors in crevice lock
dried up like river made the rhymes
to know what ocean were unkempt
or hide's detain the wean of
hide's felicity depend.

TINA DARRAGH

from *On the Corner to Off the Corner*

"oilfish" to "old chap" for "C"

Performing military service for the king and bearing a child
have a common medieval root. The progression to this point
is first academic, then technical. Textbooks give way
to textiles which lead to T-formations and T-groups.
We pause to add "th" and proceed through Mediterranean
anemia, deep seas, Greek muses, pesticides, young shoots
and the instinctual desire for death. It is there that
we find "thane" to be followed by all manner of "thanks",
including the "thank-you-ma'am"—a ridge built across a
road so rain will roll off.

"bounded" to "bower" for "E"

"Bo" is a sound bordering on "bourgeois" and fronting
for "bow wow" and "box" before the "o" in boy. The
movement between can be described either as sluggish
or patient, depending on one's bent. From sidepiece to
horsehairs, bells to vulgar, fin to front, head to hollow,
weather edge to alley, capsule to saw, nephron to spar,
the action continues alternating left to right accompanied
by the chant: "1 stick 2 head 3 hair 4 frog 5 screw."

"yea" to "yill" for "W"

The color "yellow" comes from "light bay", but whether the image refers to "light over the bay" or "light from the bay" is not certain. The definition is surrounded by trees—tulipwood, buckthorn, smoke, birch, pine, osage orange, jessamine—and suggests that we turn to the area of "far and wide" and "faraway" for further clarification.

"Oran" to "ordain" for "J"

orchestration = "he raves"

The prefix for "Ceylon trail" promises "main orange" after orbits. Flashback to "front orange" where diversities _____ a satellite then skip to "hair order" chorus, again an orbit. Down eleven, ordination is opposed to satellite, a shape end circular as in "organized vision". LEVEL also leads to a circle—"plants Ireland"— two below "beverage", one below "prehistoric." Finally, islands make "part importance" fleshy by adding "a" to orbit as orangey united to surrounding fulcrums "celestial"— Orkney, five up, Orkney.

ludicrous stick

to
clean
over: T
formal.
whip. b.
or surpass
completion or
etc.: They need
into shape. 6. 1
19) 7. lick the d
stroke of the tongue
by taken up by one str
cream cone. 10. See salt
b. a brief, brisk burst of ac
pace or clip; speed. 12. Jazz.
in swing music. 13. lick and a
perfunctory manner of doing some
time to clean thoroughly, but gave
promise. (ME lick(e), OE liccian; c.
akin toGoth (bi) laigon, L lingere, GK
(up) - licker, n.

Lick (lik), n. a ring formation in the
the face of the moon: about 21 miles in

lick er-in (lik er in), n. a roller on
chine, esp. the roller that opens the st

the card and transfers the fibers to the
Also called taker-in. (n. use of v. phra

licking (lik ing), n. 1. Informal. a.a p
thrashing. b. a reversal or disappointm
2. the act of one who or that which lic

licorice (lik e   ish, lik rish

viewing
point

ALAN DAVIES

Shared Sentences

Towards the latter days of the evening
a kind restored verbiage, a diligence
came down within, towards us.

You can choose one for life
not exactly misunderstanding obeisance
inherent in subtraction from the crowd.

An agreement is radial in this part, or
a partial and agreed seating
that circumvents the permission to answer.

Swear perseverant patience hales our times
for deconstructing quest, for sense
mixes with this appetite that makes.

Forgetting fail; nor remember to forget the insolence
of destined or desiring force
weakening these knees, our galaxy.

When with evening shuttered space or time
relaxes in our axing excellence, we tread
verbose nerves flattening our layered bed.

Or enter on translucent trust, loom
above the head; ineluctable, irrecoverably
nascent arms wane tainted at our limbs.

Recidivist tendencies in trekking devotions
harden, following elusive cues thoroughly
or dry blood's desiring to be taut.

Or evinces our entrapping sounds
in veinous closure over speech, demands
closure for these fretted hands.

A gentle proving paves us into pleading
these oblate lives; these vectoring, or
the obverse fantasy inflates to die.

The armored motion of engaging persons
seethes with reason; these outside lives
polish the line of sight we return by.

With productions of norm in sanctity, frames
elude all doing with an undone felt
securing feeling, vespers in your arms.

In returning into voices, on
claims, in thought's direct address
initialled pledges trace us to our words.

Inveterate, for reasons, loosen torsion
or pilloried high parts waste out
for losing passion, the bit that starts our heart.

Towards nor past these seen or unseen hands
with moist hierarchy bends this diligence,
starts in seating all that tested stands.

Coming, in parting this passage of time
proposes anklets for verbs, hierarchies
forming proportions, helping us home.

From deep changes with purges ablutions
rise, reach in us a pediment for speech,
this testament, a map prolonging sentiment.

Halving in effusive sentences twill veils
portend this hulled incisive self, abating
twin sails for distancing, in eyes.

Any lessening of feeling's strength,
a durable parameter, duress of being
ever in eventual caress and stasis.

Touring ardor or pacific languor talks
inventing equinox from dream, clearing head for
clarity specific language spots contain.

Never mind; these blousing anecdotes
tend within these trenchant anarchies
a penchant for more bluesy things to find.

Nascent flourishings detail our eyes
with children, nonidentical twins with certain
identical characteristics, a noun and a verb.

Fluctuant quadrants are our heros now,
the eyes discern a median their equal creasing
out of time, habitues the legs forget to fathom.

Propelling arms within these arms at rest
arrest a new dominion; proportions clauses strengthen
in contesting arrogance, lease aisles of time.

In trancing lives will linger sentience, an
obedient motion over stones that softness bends
to dust, standing vertical what horizontal lies.

Petting in a way with angled vision all occasion,
all tense, two cavalcading lives obey a fiction
in an instant, a desiring motion backing into breath.

from *Name*

If the devices fail pens
fall and begin to harvest.
This harvest. This harvest,
a part of speech,
lets us onto the thruway,
a part of a part of speech.
There are
moments when I don't see
you.
There is a time bracket
for this bill of goods.
There is a ship date and
a must release.
There is a climate changer
and a torrivent, and
four cabinet fans.

I particularly want to keep
the feathers
off the Irish blanket.
In an effort flying to
kidnap the kidnapped
victims we have flown.
There is a simple, kind
of adverbial, presence that
lets us. We are, that
we really are.
If there is an unneeded
transition, if
there is a persuasion, if,
if that takes us
into the bakelite, then:
labradorite.

We make the mistakes
in each other's speech.
We find the blonde words
in each other's
mouths.
We speak them, there.
We know the sheep
in the absent fold
and the labial folds
that absent us from sleep.
This we is a we that weep.
The two persons in the two persons
remember each other
in two small letters.
And the tall thighs in a handkerchief
are fricative
and voiced
and labial, and weak.
We can talk more
if we speak
and you can stay the night.

CARLA HARRYMAN

For She

The back of the head resting on the pillow was not wasted. We couldn't hear each other speak. The puddle in the bathroom, the sassy one. There were many years between us. I stared the stranger into facing up to Maxine, who had come out of the forest bad from wet nights. I came from an odd bed, a vermilion riot attracted to loud dogs. Nonetheless, I could pay my rent and provide for him. On this occasion she apologized. An arrangement that did not provoke inspection. Outside on the stagnant water was a motto. He more than I perhaps though younger. I sweat at amphibians, managed to get home. The sunlight from the window played up his golden curls and a fist screwed over one eye. Right to left and left to right until the sides of her body were circuits. While dazed and hidden in the room, he sang to himself, severe songs, from a history he knew nothing of. Or should I say malicious? Some rustic gravure, soppy but delicate at pause. I wavered, held her up. I tremble, jack him up. Matted wallowings, I couldn't organize the memory. Where does he find his friends? Maxine said to me, "But it was just you again." In spite of the cars and the smoke and the many languages, the radio and appliances, the flat broad buzz of the tracks, the anxiety with which the eyes move to meet the phone and all the arbitrary colors, I am just the same. Unplug the glass, face the docks. I might have been in a more simple schoolyard.

Beginning to End

for John Harryman

I used to be sure but I've forgotten how to count. Would you like something warm to drink?

Daisy mopped her brow.

Why won't you talk?

I will, later.

Sometimes I know I'm just part of a procedure. A moon moves over my head that no one else can see.

Bunchy shrubs on the roadside applauded. Ravens spread their wings while other of her animals fled from rain. Army jeeps flew down the road grinding their gears, their headlights burning into the dawn.

Daisy finished her nap but didn't wake up her friend because she didn't feel like talking. She stood in the center of the room holding her suitcase, deciding not to control her style because she didn't know if she would like the children. Someone asked if she were comfortable as if she had just woken up in the hospital.

I'm fine. I'm fine. She wanted to fix the upholstery in her car which was tearing steadily, daily.

Would you mind looking up car upholsterer in the yellow pages? I hate the condition my things fall into. Nothing is precious these days. I mean in the sense of precious things having stamina and an inconceivably long life.

She felt guilty asking someone to do something for her. If I were not young, she thought, I would be happier. The future was looking a little blank. If I had something to back me up I'd be wiser. This she knew was truer than she had understanding for, so she put it on hold. Already maturity was taking up some slack.

Her friend woke up. It looked like she had been sleeping in a hole. She rubbed her shoulder. Ouch, she said. Tomorrow I'm going to sleep someplace else.

Daisy smiled, but her friend didn't see her. You'll have to leave without me, I'm waiting for the car.

You know, I hate cars.

Yes, I do.

I'll probably miss you.

I'll probably miss you too.

A comfortable silence grew between them while they were listening to the Pacific Ocean.

Daisy, you don't have something you want.

I have everything that I want but that doesn't seem to matter. When I see something I have never seen before, I often regret being who I am, but not because of envy. I want what I'm seeing to recognize me first.

This is very complicated.

You are a dreamer, said Daisy.

You're talking to me? You make me feel plain, even when I'm wearing something fancy, if not particularly practical or dynamic. Sometimes I believe I will be real if I let go of these oddities. Well, you don't have to listen to me now, now that I have a track and a scent. It feels good just to talk.

You don't think about things very much.

You mean thing things?

Yes, those are what I mean.

I do but you weren't listening completely to me. But to the part that interests only you.

I won't take that as an attack but will continue, said Daisy. She was trying out brave determination with a bit of subtle oppression, on the one hand. She had a superstition that is was something else mysterious that would help her to really be what she was acting out. The way I see it is this. She stopped, frightened.

Her friend was thinking about how two-year-olds will speak simultaneously. She desired such ecstasy, but was critical of the arrangement among adults. She listened against her will.

I don't have a private moon, said Daisy, I have the same moon everyone has. And that is what I mean by thing. Had she not been inside, she would have gone inside, but she went outside for the same reason.

Her friend watched the flies on the other side of the screen door. Sometimes a foot would stick through.

I suppose it's better not to stand here.

What did you say? asked Daisy, opening a beer on the porch.

Nothing.

Come here.

Why?

It's hot, said Daisy, and I have spoiled everything.

Not everything.

She stopped her car in front of the ticket booth, feeling for her hat before giving a woman money for the show, then parked in the middle of the lot and waited for the sun to go down.

Expectations, the ones that were actually sickening, had the character of someone observing you doing one thing many times. A room turning into a sack of potatoes faced with the prospect of endless maintenance.

> The Guests are scatter'd thro' the land,
> For the Eye altering alters all;
> The Senses roll themselves in fear,
> And the Flat Earth becomes a Ball.

I'm not comfortable here.

I'm not either I don't think.

Sit still.

Daisy sat there trying to make sense of it. It was green at the base, as elsewhere. When they arrived at the rodeo, the thing she noticed most was the volcano above them. It had been the first thing she noticed in the rearview mirror backing out the driveway. A drove of cows stumbled into the arena. Cowboys on horseback and cowgirls on foot followed. Cowboys roped the cows and cowgirls milked them. A cow broke a leg. The drunken audience restrained its tears. Then the storm broke and people went to their cars.

This, said Daisy, is some fate. In fact, it could be just like any fate and that is exactly the problem with it.

The best story, said Walt, is about someone's life from the beginning to the end.

What are you talking about?

Biography.

Only, I think, said Daisy, if the life is long. Let's go someplace where I can hear what you're saying.

Do you have something in mind?

That is not the point, said Daisy. There is always the possibility of inventing a new system of education.

If, said Walt, something gets too large, one stops seeing the details, and I believe now is a perfect example of what I'm talking about.

Oh?

Then again, I am often hungrier than I look.

Everybody I know, said Daisy, is hungrier than they look.

But I am not talking about everybody.

Yes, you are talking about yourself.

And that is the point on which we differ.

When Daisy was with Walt she saw herself as other people. Other people with him too. This was confusing but she understood its *raison d'etre*. She loved to be around an intelligent person and say the same thing to him that she could imagine someone else would say. She tried to make herself someone else because she thought it would amuse him.

All this was together in one place. She was standing on top of a weakling, a little jelly earth.

Am I standing on another tier, or is this where I was born?

Not here son, said an ecclesiastical looking man.

Are you religious?

Not too, are you?

Am I what?

We were talking about this place, these flatlands, said the man. Pebbly paths leading through a treeless habitation, then beyond the town of shacks and stores in the opposite direction where everything feels the same but slowly turns into a cemetery. Out here men and women stand shoulder to shoulder in a state of grace. This society might be characterized as a standing ovation simultaneously in mourning.

We came from a small outpost in Chile (the people in the world you're in now are so familiar with all the countries they could own them but instead display them like a pack of cards). Everything there was brown except the dyed garments, drapes, rugs, etc., of the population who hated drabness and believed they lived in a society coated in brown because of a curse. Their way of cooking became convoluted. Who knows if it worked? They also believed they were cursed by a second spirit, because the demon who made them dwell in drabness was completely characterless, and if there was anything else they hated it was characterlessness. They were being falsely represented at any rate and there was basically nothing to be done. If you want to know *why* I'm telling you this you'll have to ask my father.

So, they went to the mountains made out of white granite. They lay down on some rocks, glowed in the blue sky and died. But they didn't really die, they came here. And I am one of them and we are detached from strife. We'll tell you all about it if you will bear us some children. Our only problem is we are childless because our seeds will grow only in foreign ground to speak euphemistically, all things being equal as I see it. Here comes father.

Hello father.

Hello boy. Hello woman.

Hello, said Daisy, I'm sure I've gone too far.

Not at all. There is nothing to separate us.

Would you please take me to the nursery?

What for?

I want plants to move to the country.

I lived in the country once and that's enough, said Walt.

I was just making an excuse, said Daisy. Let's go home. Oh it is sad to be in one place all the time. But that's not why I'm compulsive. It is the possibility of transformation.

I've been reading theories on kinship, Walt said to change the conversation. Then he stopped the car to take a picture of an old church.

DIANE WARD

Approximately

meaning a context or vision to confer with this which could be a
book.
meaning what I just said confers with this but a licking sound.
Amplified and forming an idea far from original.
A distance which becomes whimsical tension.
For instance, then an origin, an image a fantasy becomes ironic;
at home.
Flat as you once thought a centering unlike mysteries in your
imagining an animal.
Difference in eye levels.
Difference in relation and system.
Elevating a problem in placement face and in which direction.
A metal square gradually marked.
A metal square which is confrontational engaging.
Off into intensity which is hard to concentrate.
Two of the spaces of words with their own containment each
of eighty directions.
Two aesthetics granting activity value without practical functions.
Following the implied direction of possessions, environment is a
room more specific a person.
You said something visual versus a thought you were attacking.
You said change/cigarettes versus intimate intricate and which is
more interesting.
Later a time motions are visual or visualizations which translate
objects
into words.
A mass of timid outlines to each rigid color.
A mass of smiles destroys a given warmth.
Without only a loneliness to cherish.

More specific a conversation hopefully beginning now.

More specific the toxic and poison contributed to a phrase now
dated and like a date benign.

Respectable ideas are random, laying low or following up so
forget what I just said or I think.

Impossible only an advancing of thoughts their elements and
results.

No worth for what they're saying or value exists for this.

It's fine that it brings tears to your eyes or doesn't.

It's probably fine that what moves you is below you or not above
you.

Formulas to constrict imagination to a mind what it's saying
thinking and what you want its direction.

For this there's an age to define as urgent as people.

For this habit a catchy title like *musings handfuls.*

More points exist around which become you than are not.

Ends based on emotional gusts; the hands are yours that wish to
hold.

Ends as a pivotal screen viewing concealed metaphors for beauty.

What the question value in days formulated frequent written
words weeks.

I don't know an arching sounding around us.

I don't know where movements standing pointing as vacuum.

Where the word which wasn't interesting belongs as redefinition.

Where speed replaces the idea and becomes it.

Internal is categorically beautiful bombing as we expected them
whole sentences erupt up and fall.

Headlong, concrete piece by concrete piece a sight or irrational
pleasure.

Heading away to detail and immediacy.

Another form is untouchable and moves a cage into softness.

A wooden syntax of shadow forms a pillar of its own.

A highly syntax confusing both image and word and detail and
notation.

A shape which is rounded off so that corners fall away.

Blank and another ordering attention paying off.

Blank intensity stares.

The Habit Of Energy

An enthusiastic gummed flap, awaiting. Something cloudy in the head the imitation of situation in a passive voice the pleasure-journalism of this is making a slave of pleasure and each breath is to characterize pleasure excessive and elusive, a costume of matching parts whose physical culture is caught in photographs and other aggressive forms of communication to be enlarged, a demanding optimism of perfect lips or different lips or the feeling of being different lips confused with a great person or a great town without prohibiting intensity and this, engraved on wooden blocks, multiplied and destroyed. Freedom from ignorance, a magnet in the motor that threatens to pull the forward from behind the instinct that calls attention to silence and order a number four over easy a burst of yellow that becomes its own force and resistance at the same time adjusted to speed disconnected to a great power. The claw of security and elegance pivoting on axes at right angles to each other in shadowy uniforms which mount the walls and become shadows and ghosts with powerful nervous giggles, a thin film of thrill and thrill snatched suddenly an idle habit of energy, a moment.

Tender Arc

for Chris Hauty

Describe porcelain and I was touching the cool gleam of white
    sink.
The ellipses you mention, panting, eyes call such and such to
    your heart, sighting pink, and pink settles all around me.
I can tear off pages of this notebook and still be here.

Like fantasies airing out, another in stages, runaround kiss: I
    float, a crooked video feeling, mirror for mirror.

Numbers aren't relevant: my weight goes quickly sometimes.

If you fumble, smart and resplendent, finally saturating the
    moment into a fixed home, lies-insipid go wherever you
    follow, behind you, then you're gone.

I'm alone, my clothes are the imploding kind, the kind left
    behind then duplicated.

A car idles like my sound, a drone tying multiple knots that
    are sobering, consonant ideas that find everness bound in
    one moment's soothing.

I'm starting to feel what the night is, dark and stars.

Your arm reaches through meaning touches the kindness that
    misses its mark, only to return trailing sharp corners that
    follow in a tender arc.

I appropriate pristine patches from what you've lived, from
    memories that fade and soften in you.

Elongated theories of tens secrete zeros that latch on to
    definitions made temporary by growth. Where there's one
    there'll be two.

I'm taking these on in my own memory though they belong in
    yours exactly.

Man-made cases of please, continue. Titles for You: phone an
    enemy, low play, keeping stronger pinned to your chest
    like facts that stack better flatter.

There are sunglasses, it's hot. A fashion like fungus passes
    through the usual motions of fit then rot.

It's the church, its green door the same color as the blue sky,
    its white walls the same as the brown dust.

Murmuring, something I knew from then, scheme or order, a
    sort of maimed invective, passed so high. I fit better, I bite,
    my aim is grounded in utterance.

The serious one seduces me, near and coupled with Sunday's
    reasoning in you, still, without the motioning and
    fleeting, barely moving.

In one, you stand in an old church's doorway.

Run through the place where your hand on the cold wood is
    encouraged, temperament stored away.
In one, you're beating a clump of seaweed with a stick or a
    rock or a shell.
Run forward, retrieve the dream that flickered to a stop when
    the machine fell.
In the dark, it didn't matter how they looked.
One part, an instant antonym overpowers your disdain for
    embellishment, lazy hook.
Once a man fell asleep in his lover's closet, obsessed with the
    smell and feel of the empty clothes.
Come and shelter us, creeping minutes cover content,
    interesting but melting away. The important finishing
    rose.
I've seen them all lying around off of you and I don't equate
    them to you.
Reams of paper, calls, minor sounds distorted in your mood,
    its plan, simple: over fate, to face it like a friend you could
    lose.
No shirt. No opinion or lingering out of courtesy.
In one you wear a bathing suit, one shorts, one pants with a
    belt.
Comfort and care, I pace myself and lose, one contortion, one
    stance, hasty minutes mean more when refelt.
In two, you wear shoes. Invent loosened humor as you share,
    keep laments at arm's length, the nuisance.
Sky is in all three. Light spins above calm, free from
    atmosphere.
Two are on the beach, the water's blue, sky just as blue.
The pair of aimless figures drone like doves that reel high
    against the humble, muted sky.
Your voice before or after the camera, were you yelling over
    sounds around you and what sounds.
Our choices create scores like basketball, the fans hurl loose,
    intelligent phone messages and hound us then sometime
    we lose what we found.

In Mexico, a secure photograph is one without history.

You would let me over the fence, my fingers scraping the paint
   off, then I would be sure that the laughter comes mixed
   with bliss and fury.

But what I know. Covered in crossed fingers, heart and soul.

Each of you in Mexico. Each of me, blue sins accepted.

With me, three photographs are here. Picking off the if and
   then each season, steam and blacktop facts.

It's dark, I know it's there, but I can't see the clock.

Parking lots may surround you, odors, hints that once were
   cherished, untitled mansions that never got their start.

Mid-afternoon, from across the river, buildings around Wall
   Street throw shadows onto each other, colors vary as the
   "shadowed" buildings' colors change. Permanently paint
   the shadows on.

A still patch of room, hum outside, sliver of filtered sounds
   across the wall, the sheets grow hollow, one you threw
   over, the other under where you hover and carry last
   night's phantom, still dream, memory stage. You learned
   the faint phrase low voices travel on.

The unfinished skyscraper downtown twinkling lights
   eternally.

I could diminish. My title is my name and a frown pounded
   from the hardest ink stings the sight we purchased.

In the dark, a big clock. Minutes marked by figures held in a
   strange hand.

This is my view: another apartment window, shelves and
   sugar.

Or then this is you, just summer, a carbon sentiment, intro to
   yellower fields, just tugging, just far.

Prosperity

mention trusty as a talk of marching, orders.
this one earful is longing and last. Metered
unclubbable room full of people who lean
away, float above whose arms reach to grab
this *me* M-menace. As an old friend potential
        penance. Leveled to conditions' respite
lay once on softness, unsounded.
Walk up on toes as if entering his own mentor
and glamorous hallucinated argument. How much would it cost
    to say, sail under false colors.
And long to juxtapose this word to circulate
from the fragments of its belonging together.
Hand you this value or not, I'm necessarily alone,
not to obligate a gentle person.
Response fused with understatement, descendant dramatics
that's what it means to be American, So Long.
This word, her, even ever post-exist in your mind?
Or deviate from its mention, in three sections
        collapsible normal.
Pass illogically from here, acute angel-types
a sphere containing requests: your right to try
for technically imperfect regeneration.

Bibliographical Information

JACKSON MAC LOW (1922). *The Twin Plays* (New York: Mac Low & Bloedow, 1963; 2nd ed., New York: Something Else, 1966); *The Pronouns—A Collection of 40 Dances—For the Dancers* (New York: Mac Low, 1964; 2nd ed., revised, London: Tetrad, 1971; 3rd ed., newly revised, Barrytown, NY: Station Hill, 1979); *Verdurous Sanguinaria* (Baton Rouge, LA: Southern University, 1967); *August Light Poems* (New York: Caterpillar, 1967); *22 Light Poems* (Los Angeles: Black Sparrow, 1968); *23rd Light Poem: For Larry Eigner* (London: Tetrad, 1969); *Stanzas for Iris Lezak* (Barton, VT: Something Else, 1972); *4 trains* (Providence, RI: Burning Deck, 1974); *36th Light Poem: In Memoriam Buster Keaton* (London: Permanent Press, 1975); *21 Matched Asymmetries* (London: Aloes, 1978); *54th Light Poem: For Ian Tyson* (Milwaukee: Membrane, 1978); *A Dozen Douzains for Eve Rosenthal* (Toronto: Gronk, 1978); *phone* (New York and Amsterdam: Printed Editions and Kontexts, 1979); *Asymmetries 1–260* (New York: Printed Editions, 1980); *"Is That Wool Hat My Hat?"* (Milwaukee: Membrane, 1982); *From Pearl Harbor Day to FDR's Birthday* (College Park, MD: Sun & Moon Press, 1982); *Bloomsday* (Barrytown, NY: Station Hill, 1984); *French Sonnets* (Tucson, AZ: Black Mesa Press/Chax Press, 1984); *The Virginia Woolf Poems* (Providence, RI: Burning Deck, 1985); *Representative Works: 1938-1985* (New York: Roof, 1986).

HANNAH WEINER (1928). *The Magritte Poems* (Sacramento, CA: Poetry News Letter, 1970); *Sun June 9* (Providence, RI: Diana's Bi-Monthly, 1975); *Clairvoyant Journal 1974* (New York: Angel Hair, 1978); *Little Books/Indians* (New York: Roof, 1980); *Nijole's House* (Elmwood, CT: Potes & Poets Press, 1981); *Code Poems* (Barrytown, NY: Open Book [Station Hill], 1982); *Sixteen* (Windsor, VT: Awede Press, 1983); *Spoke* (Washington, DC: Sun & Moon Press, 1984). *Written IN/the 01* (Victoria, Australia: Post Neo, 1985).

SUSAN HOWE (1937). *Hinge Picture* (New York: Telephone Books, 1974); *The Western Borders* (Willits, CA: Tuumba Press, 1976); *Secret History of the Dividing Line* (New York: Telephone Books, 1978); *Cabbage Gardens* (Chicago, IL: Fathom Press, 1979); *The Liberties* (Guilford, CT: Loon Books, 1980); *Pythagorean Silence* (New York: Montemora Foundation, 1982); *Defenestration of Prague* (New York: Kulchur Foundation, 1983); *My Emily Dickinson* (Berkeley, CA: North Atlantic Books, 1985); *Articulation of Sound Forms in Time* (Windsor, VT: Awede Press, 1986).

CLARK COOLIDGE (1939). *Flag Flutter & U.S. Electric* (New York: Lines, 1966); *Clark Coolidge* (New York: Lines, 1967); *Ing* (New York: Angel Hair, 1968); *Space* (New York: Harper & Row, 1970); *The So* (New York: Adventures in Poetry, 1971); *Suite V* (New York: Adventures in Poetry, 1973); *The Maintains* (San Francisco: This, 1974); *Polaroid* (New York and Bolinas, CA: Adventures in Poetry and Big Sky, 1975); *Quartz Hearts* (San Francisco: This, 1978); *Own Face* (Lenox, MA: Angel Hair, 1978); *Smithsonian Depositions/Subject To a Film* (New York: Vehicle Editions, 1980); *American Ones* (Bolinas, CA: Tombouctou, 1981); *A Geology* (Needham, MA: Potes & Poets Press, 1981); *Research* (Berkeley, CA: Tuumba Press, 1982); *Mine: The One That Enters the Stories* (Berkeley, CA: The Figures, 1982); *The Crystal Text* (Great Barrington, MA: The Figures, 1986); *Solution Passage: Poems 1978–1981* (Los Angeles: Sun & Moon Press, 1986).

LYN HEJINIAN (1941). *A Thought Is the Bride of What Thinking* (Willits, CA: Tuumba Press, 1976); *A Mask of Motion* (Providence, RI: Burning Deck, 1977); *Gesualdo* (Berkeley, CA: Tuumba Press, 1978); *Writing Is An Aid to Memory* (Great Barrington, MA: The Figures, 1978); *My Life* (Providence, RI: Burning Deck, 1980); *Redo* (Grenada, MS: Salt-Works Press, 1984); *The Guard* (Berkeley, CA: Tuumba Press, 1984).

TED GREENWALD (1942). *Lapstrake* (New York: Lines, 1964); *Short Sleeves* (Ithaca, N.Y.: Buffalo Press, 1969); *No Eating* (Paris: Blue Pig Press, 1971); *Somewhere in Ho* [with Ed. Baynard] (New York: Buffalo Press, 1972); *Making a Living* (New York: Adventures in Poetry, 1973); *The New Money* (Paris: Blue Pig Press, 1973); *Makes Sense* (New York: Angel Hair, 1973); *Miami* (Bowling Green, OH: Doones Press, 1975); *Native Land* (Washington, D.C.: Titanic Books, 1977); *You Bet!* (San Francisco: This, 1978); *Common Sense* (Kensington, CA: L Publications, 1978); *Licorice Chronicles* (New York: Kulchur Foundation, 1979); *Use No Hooks* (New York: Asylum's Press, 1980); *Smile* (Berkeley, CA: Tuumba Press, 1981); *Exit the Face* (New York: Museum of Modern Art, 1982); *Word of Mouth* (Los Angeles: Sun & Moon Press, 1986).

PETER SEATON (1942). *Agreement* (New York: Asylum's Press, 1978); *The Son Master* (New York: Roof, 1982); *Crisis Intervention* (Berkeley, CA: Tuumba Press, 1983).

MICHAEL PALMER (1943). *Plan of the City of O* (Boston: Barn Dream Press, 1971); *Blake's Newton* (Los Angeles: Black Sparrow Press, 1972); *C's Songs* (Albany, CA: Sand Dollar, 1973); *Six Poems* (Los Angeles, CA: Black Sparrow, 1973); *The Circular Gates* (Los Angeles: Black Sparrow Press, 1974); *Without Music* (Santa Barbara: Black Sparrow Press, 1977); *Transparency of the Mirror* (Albany, CA: Little Dinosaur, 1980); *Alogon* (Berkeley, CA: Tuumba Press, 1980); *Notes for Echo Lake* (San Francisco: North Point Press, 1981); *First Figure* (San Francisco: North Point Press, 1984).

RAY DI PALMA (1943). *Max* (Iowa City: The Body Press, 1969); *Macaroons* [with Stephen Shrader] (Bowling Green, OH: Doones, 1969); *Between the Shapes* (East Lansing, MI: Zeitgeist Press, 1970); *The Gallery Goers* (Ithaca, NY: Ithaca House, 1971); *All Bowed Down* (Providence, RI: Burning Deck, 1972); *Works In a Drawer* (Bowling Green, OH: Blue Chair Press, 1972); *Borgia Circles* (Northampton, MA: Sand Project Press, 1972); *Time Being* [with Asa Benveniste and Tom Raworth] (London: Trigram Press, 1972); *Soli* (Ithaca, NY: Ithaca House, 1974); *Sargasso Transcries* (Bowling Green, OH: 'X' Editions, 1974); *Max/A Sequel* (Providence, RI: Burning Deck, 1974); *Accidental Interludes* (Providence, RI: Turkey Press, 1975); *Marquee* (New York: Asylum's Press, 1977); *Cuiva Sails* (College Park, MD: Sun & Moon Press, 1978); *Planh* (New York: Casement Books, 1979); *Observatory Gardens* (Berkeley, CA: Tuumba Press, 1979); *Genesis* (Toronto: Underwhich Editions, 1980); *Labyrinth Radio* (New York: Case Books, 1981); *23 Works* (Berlin: Edition Vogelsang, 1982); *13 Works* (Berlin: Edition Vogelsang, 1982); *Two Poems* (Windsor, VT: Awede Press, 1982); *Chan* (New York: One of Ten, 1984); *January Zero* (West Branch, IA: Coffee House Press, 1984); *Startle Luna* (New York: Sleight of Hand Books, 1984).

JAMES SHERRY (1946). *Part Songs* (New York: Roof, 1978); *In Case* (College Park, MD: Sun & Moon Press, 1981); *Converses* (Windsor, VT: Awede Press, 1982); *Popular Fiction* (New York: Roof, 1985); *The Word I Like White Paint Considered* (Windsor, VT: Awede Press, 1986).

RAE ARMANTROUT (1947). *Extremities* (Berkeley, CA: The Figures, 1978); *The Invention of Hunger* (Berkeley, CA: Tuumba Press, 1979); *Precedence* (Providence, RI: Burning Deck, 1985).

P. INMAN (1947). *What Happens Next* (Washington, DC: Some of Us Press, 1974); *Platin* (College Park, MD: Sun & Moon Press, 1979); *Ocker* (Berkeley, CA: Tuumba Press, 1982); *Uneven Development* (Oakland, CA: Jimmy's House of Knowledge, 1984); *Think of One* (Needham, MA: Potes & Poets Press, 1987).

BOB PERELMAN (1947). *Braille* (Ithaca, NY: Ithaca House, 1975); *7 Works* (Berkeley, CA: The Figures, 1978); *a. k. a.* [parts I and II] (Berkeley, CA: Tuumba Press, 1979); *Primer* (San Francisco: This, 1981); *a. k. a.* (Great Barrington, MA: The Figures, 1984); *To the Reader* (Berkeley, CA: Tuumba Press, 1984); *The First World* (Great Barrington, MA: The Figures, 1986)

BRUCE ANDREWS (1948). *Edge* (Washington, DC: Some of Us Press, 1973); *Appalachia* (Yellow Springs, OH: Pellet Press, 1973); *A Cappella* (East Lansing, MI: Ghost Dance, 1973); *Corona* (Providence, RI:

Burning Deck, 1974); *Vowels* (Washington, D.C.: O Press); *Film Noir* (Providence, RI: Burning Deck, 1978); *Praxis* (Berkeley, CA: Tuumba Press, 1978); *Jeopardy* (Windsor, VT: Awede, 1980); *Sonnets—Memento Mori* (San Francisco: This, 1980); *R + B* (New York, Segue, 1981); *Love Songs* (Baltimore: Pod Books, 1982); *Wobbling* (New York: Roof, 1981); *Excommunicate* (Hartford, CT: Potes and Poets Press, 1982); *Give Em Enough Rope* (Los Angeles: Sun & Moon Press, 1986).

BARRETT WATTEN (1948). *Opera—Works* (Bolinas, CA: Big Sky, 1975); *Decay* (San Francisco: This, 1977); *Plasma/Paralles/"X"* (Berkeley, CA: Tuumba Press, 1979); *1–10* (San Francisco: This, 1980); *Complete Thought* (Berkeley, CA: Tuumba Press, 1982); *Total Syntax* (Carbondale: Southern Illinois University Press, 1985); *Progress* (New York: Roof, 1985); *Conduit* (San Francisco: Gaz, 1986).

CHARLES BERNSTEIN (1950). *Parsing* (New York: Asylum's Press, 1976); *Shade* (College Park, MD: Sun & Moon Press, 1978); *Poetic Justice* (Baltimore: Pod Books, 1979); *Disfrutes* (Peter Ganick, 1979; new ed., Needham, MA: Potes & Poets Press, 1981); *Senses of Responsibility* (Berkeley, CA: Tuumba Press, 1979); *Controlling Interests* (New York: Roof, 1980); *The Occurrence of Tune* [with Susan Bee (Laufer)] (New York: Segue, 1981); *Stigma* (Barrytown, N.Y.: Station Hill, 1981); *Islets/Irritations* (New York: Jordan Davies, 1983); *Content's Dream: Essays* (Los Angeles: Sun & Moon Press, 1986); *The Sophist* (Los Angeles: Sun & Moon Press, 1986).

TINA DARRAGH (1950). *my hands   to myself* (Washington, DC: Dry Imager, 1976); *Pi in the Skye* (Ferguson & Franzino, 1980); *on the corner to off the corner* (College Park, MD: Sun & Moon Press, 1981).

ALAN DAVIES (1951). *slough cup hope tantrum* (Boston: Other Publications, 1975); *Split Thighs* (Boston: Other Publications, 1976); *a an av es* (Needham, MA: Potes & Poets Press, 1981); *Abuttal* (New York: Casement Books, 1982); *Mnemonotechnics* (Needham, MA: Potes & Poets Press, 1982); *Active 24 Hours* (New York: Roof, 1982); *Name* (San Francisco: This, 1986).

CARLA HARRYMAN (1952). *Percentage* (Berkeley, CA: Tuumba Press, 1979); *Under the Bridge* (San Francisco: This, 1980); *Property* (Berkeley, CA: Tuumba Press, 1982); *The Middle* (San Francisco: Gaz, 1983); *Vice* (Needham, MA: Potes & Poets Press, 1986).

DIANE WARD (1956). *Trop-I-Dom* (Washington, DC: Jawbone, 1977); *The Light American* (Washington, DC: Jawbone, 1979); *Theory of Emotion* (New York: Segue/O Press, 1979); *Never Without One* (New York: Roof, 1984).

Collaborative Work:

Bruce Andrews, Charles Bernstein, Ray DiPalma, Steve McCaffery, and
  Ron Silliman, *Legend* (New York: L=A=N=G=U=A=G=E/Segue,
  1980)

Selected Journals:

Joglars (ed. by Clark Coolidge and Michael Palmer) 1964-65
Tottel's (ed. by Ron Silliman) 1970-
This (ed. by Barrett Watten and Robert Grenier) 1971-73; (ed. by Barrett
  Watten) 1974-82
L (ed. by Curtis Faville) 1972-74
Shirt (ed. by Ray DiPalma) 1973
Hills (ed. by Bob Perelman) 1973-83
Eel (ed. by P. Inman) 1974-77
A Hundred Posters (ed. by Alan Davies) 1976-82
Sun & Moon: A Journal of Literature & Art (ed. by Douglas Messerli)
  1976-82
Roof (ed. by James Sherry) 1976-79
Paper Air (ed. by Gil Ott) 1976-
Vanishing Cab (ed. by Jerry Estrin) 1976-
Miam (ed. by Tom Mandel) 1977-78
Dog City (ed. by The Poetry Factory [participants in the Washington,
  DC "Folio Books group"]) 1977-80
L=A=N=G=U=A=G=E (ed. by Bruce Andrews and Charles Bernstein)
  1978-81
E-Pod (ed. by Kirby Malone and Marshall Reese) 1978-80
QU (ed. by Carla Harryman) 1979-
The Difficulties (ed. by Tom Beckett) 1980-
Poetics Journal (ed. by Lyn Hejinian and Barrett Watten) 1982-
Jimmy & Lucy's House of "K" (ed. by Andrew Schelling and Benjamin
  Friedlander) 1983-
Temblor (ed. by Leland Hickman) 1985-
Ottotole (ed. by Michael Amnasan and Gail Sher) 1985-

The above journals represent publications that committed themselves
extensively to "Language" writing and/or were edited by poets included

in this anthology. Many other journals of the period, including *0-9*, *Big Sky*, *The World*, *Big Deal*, *Bezoar*, *La-bas*, *Slit Wrist*, *Unnatural Acts*, *Flora Danica*, *Terraplane*, *United Artists*, *Sulfur*, *O.ARS*, *Box Car*, *Oink!*, *How(ever)*, *Acts*, *Splash* [New Zealand], *Reality Studios* [Great Britain], *Writing* [Canada], and *Pessimistic Labor* have served as forums and references for some of these poets.

Anthology Selections:

Bruce Andrews and Michael Wiater, eds., "The Andrews/Wiater Issue," *Toothpick, Lisbon, and the Orcas Islands*, 3, no. 1 (Fall 1973).

Ron Silliman, ed., "The Dwelling Place: 9 Poets," *Alcheringa*, n.s., 1, no. 2 (1975).

Steve McCaffery, ed., "The Politics of the Referent," *Open Letter*, 3rd series, no. 7 (Summer 1977).

Ron Silliman, ed., "A Clark Coolidge Symposium," *Stations*, no. 5 (Winter 1978).

Bob Perelman, ed., *Talks, Hills*, nos. 6/7 (Spring 1980).

Ron Silliman, ed., "Realism: An Anthology of 'Language' Writing." *Ironwood*. no. 20 (1982), 61-142.

Charles Bernstein, ed., "Language Sampler," *Paris Review*, no. 86 (Winter 1983), 75-125.

Michael Palmer, ed., *Code of Signals: Recent Writings in Poetics* (Io. no. 3) Berkeley, CA: North Atlantic Books, 1983).

Bruce Andrews and Charles Bernstein, ed., *The L=A=N=G=U=A=G=E Book* (Carbondale: Southern Illinois University Press, 1985).

Bob Perelman, ed., *Writing/Talks* (Carbondale: Southern Illinois University Press, 1985).

Ron Silliman, ed., *In the American Tree: Language, Poetry, Realism* (Orono, ME: National Poetry Foundation, 1986).

Charles Bernstein, ed., "43 Poets (1984)," *boundary 2*, 14, no. 6 (1986).

Group Translations:

Jean-Pierre Faye, trans.; introduction, "Poesie language USA," by Nanos Valaoritis, *L'espace Amerique*, in *Change* (March 1981).

Claude Royet-Journoud and Emmanuel Hocquard, eds., *Vingt et un poetes americains* (Montpellier, France: Delta, 1986).